Uncle John's
IMPOSSIBLE
QUESTIONS
& Astounding Answers

By the
Bathroom ~
J~

Bathroo~ ~ess
Ashlan~ ~gon

UNCLE JOHN'S
IMPOSSIBLE QUESTIONS
& ASTOUNDING ANSWERS

For information, write:
The Bathroom Readers' Institute, P.O. Box 1117, Ashland, OR 97520
www.bathroomreader.com • 888-488-4642

Cover design by Michael Brunsfeld, San Rafael, CA
(*Brunsfeldo@comcast.net*)
Escher duckie pattern by Rob Davis (*boingloid@gmail.com*)

ISBN-13: 978-1-60710-236-6 / ISBN-10: 1-60710-236-6

Library of Congress Cataloging-in-Publication Data

Uncle John's bathroom reader impossible questions and astounding answers.
    p. cm.
ISBN 978-1-60710-236-6 (pbk.)
1. Questions and answers. 2. Curiosities and wonders.
I. Bathroom Readers' Institute (Ashland, Or.)

AG195.U5 2011
081.02'07—dc22

                                    2011006095

Second Printing
2 3 4 5 15 14 13 12

CONTENTS

THANK YOU!

The Bathroom Readers' Institute sincerely thanks the people whose advice and assistance made this book possible.

Gordon Javna

Jay Newman

Amy Miller

Jack Mingo

Michael Kerr

Brian Boone

Jeff Altemus

Angela Kern

Claire Breen

Melinda Allman

Kim Griswell

John Dollison

Thom Little

Michael Brunsfeld

Rob Davis

Mustard Press

Monica Maestas

JoAnn Padgett

Amy Ly

Annie Lam

Ginger Winters

Jennifer Frederick

Sydney Stanley

R.R. Donnelley,
who always do
the impossible

Publishers Group West

Raincoast Books

Jack Barry

Art Fleming

Loaf Newman

Madison
(the radio star, not the
mermaid from *Splash*)

Question Mark &
the Mysterians

Eddie Deezen

Thomas Crapper

IMPOSSIBLE?

Okay, we lied.

Now that we've got your attention, we should let you know that not all of the questions in *Impossible Questions* are necessarily "impossible." As Uncle John's mom used to tell him, nothing's impossible. And some readers might be familiar with a few of these astounding answers. But unless you happen to be 1)_____ (*Jeopardy!*'s all-time highest earner), 2)_____ (the brilliant scientist/violinist who bequeathed the rights to his name to a foreign university), or 3)_____ (the book publisher whom party guests always find annoying), most of these questions will probably stump you.

How do we know? Because most of them stumped us. And that's why we wrote this book—because the writers at the Bathroom Readers' Institute are always trying to stump each other with weird and obscure trivia questions, so now we're letting you in on the fun.

Here's how we do it at the BRI: We find little-known aspects of well-known information and turn them into Q&A's. For example, most people know that the Pilgrims boarded the *Mayflower* in 1620 and sailed to the New World, but how many people know what the ship *smelled* like? Another example: You probably know that an airplane was the first *machine* to break the sound barrier, but what was the first man-made *object* that surpassed the speed of sound? Here's one more: What do you have 100 more of now than you did when you were a baby? You'll find the answers to these and hundreds more in the pages of this book.

In the making of *Impossible Questions*, we did what we've been doing in *Bathroom Readers* for 25 years: Telling brief
stories that will inform, surprise, and entertain you. Bonus: When you're done reading, you can stump *your* friends!

So have fun.

And as aways,

Go with the Flow!

—Uncle John and the BRI staff

p.s. We're already gathering ideas for *Impossible Questions 2*, so if you think *you* can stump Uncle John, send your questions and answers to us by logging on to *www.bathroomreader.com*.

Answers to the three blanks on the previous page:

1) **Brad Rutter**, with total earnings of $3,370,102. (Ken Jennings holds the record for most consecutive wins—74.)

2) **Albert Einstein**. He left his name to Hebrew University of Jerusalem, who trademarked it and reportedly makes $10 million from licensing fees annually.

3) **Uncle John**.

ORIGINS

Everything has to begin somewhere.
So let's get started!

Say That Ten Times Fast

When *Kleinkinderbeschäftigungsanstalt*
didn't catch on, its inventor changed
its name to…what?

☞

Family Affair

Al, Alf, Charles, Henry, and John are
better known by their last name.
What is it?

☞

Say That Ten Times Fast

German educator Friedrich Froebel changed it to
Kindergarten, which means "children's garden." His
original term, *Kleinkinderbeschäftigungsanstalt*, meant
"institute of care, playing, and activity for small children." The idea dates to 1837, when Froebel opened
the first Kindergarten in Germany as a way to prepare
children for later grades. Froebel believed young kids
learned faster if they participated in educational activities, so his innovative curriculum combined artwork
and play with formal instruction. Froebel's idea was
so good that his "children's gardens" are still going
strong today.

Family Affair

Ringling. The five original Ringling brothers—Al,
Alf, Charles, Henry, and John—formed a traveling
performance troupe in 1884 and were soon outgross-
ing all the other small circuses in the midwestern
United States. Advertising themselves as "Ringling
Bros. United Monster Shows, Great Double Circus,
Royal European Menagerie, Museum, Caravan, and
Congress of Trained Animals," they became so successful that in 1907 they bought out their biggest
competitor—Barnum & Bailey—to create what they
called the "Greatest Show on Earth." There were
seven Ringling brothers in all—the five who founded
the circus, and two who joined later, Gus and Otto.
(They also had a sister named Ida.)

Cash Cows

What well-known maker of fun stuff
began as the Schwarzschild &
Sulzberger meat-packing company?
(And what does it have to do
with Tom Hanks?)

Ahead of Her Time

19th-century stage actress Sarah Bernhardt
popularized what women's fashion item?
(And what does it have to do
with Harrison Ford?)

☞

Cash Cows

In 1915 an executive named Thomas E. Wilson was tasked by a division of Schwarzschild & Sulzberger, a meat-packing company, to solve a problem: Find a way to sell useless byproducts from their slaughter-houses (lips, intestines, and so on) that couldn't be made into sausage or pet food. When Wilson arrived, the plant was already using sheep intestines to make surgical sutures and violin strings, but the excess animal parts were piling up. So what did he do to turn it around? He focused on sporting goods and changed the name to Wilson. His first big contract: the Chicago Cubs.

Wilson Sporting Goods has since changed hands several times. In 2000 the company achieved Hollywood immortality when one of its volleyballs co-starred alongside Tom Hanks in *Cast Away*.

Ahead of Her Time

The "divine Sarah," as Bernhardt was called, had an acting career that spanned from 1862 to 1922. Her worldwide celebrity and "silver voice" turned everything she touched into gold—including the creased, brimmed hat she wore in the 1882 French play *Fédora*. Through the 1920s, the fedora hat was a staple of women's fashion; it became popular with men in the 1930s.

In 1981 Harrison Ford gave the fedora new life as the hat of choice for Nazi-fighting archaeologists.

— ORIGINS —

Das Boots

Two brothers.

Two Nazis.

Two rival shoe companies.

Who were the brothers?

And what were their shoes?

Das Boots

Not long after World War I, two cobbler brothers, Adolf and Rudolf Dassler, started *Gebrüder Dassler Schuhfabrik* (Dassler Brothers Shoe Factory) in the town of Herzogenaurach, Bavaria. In 1933 the brothers joined Hitler's Nazi party. Of the two, Rudolph, who went by Rudi, was the more ardent Nazi, and a rift began to form between them. When World War II broke out, Rudi joined the military, while Adolf, who went by Adi, stayed behind to manufacture boots and weapons for the German army.

After the war, tensions between the brothers grew worse. Rudi was arrested by American occupation forces, and he believed that Adi had reported him as a member of the SS. Adi denied it, but after Rudi was released, he quit the company and opened his own shoe factory across town.

Adi Dassler combined his first and last names to name his shoe company "adidas" (all lowercase); Rudi did the same and named his company Ruda (later changed to Puma). The brothers never spoke again, and their bitter rivalry split the town into competing factions separated by the Aurach River. Said one local resident: "You'd always tend to look at the shoes a person is wearing before you strike up a conversation."

Footnote: Although the Dassler brothers were Nazis, they provided running shoes for African-American track star Jesse Owens in the 1936 Olympics. Owens won four gold medals that year…and put the Dasslers on the map as expert athletic shoemakers.

It's Watching You Right Now

A California man named David Hampton was unimpressed with the Tamagotchi. "You can't pet it," he complained. So he invented his own version, which ended up getting banned from the National Security Agency's headquarters. What did he invent?

☞

Toy Story

What fictional version of a real toy— first released in 1938—suddenly became popular in 1983?

☞

It's Watching You Right Now

Hampton invented the Furby, an interactive toy robot that's part owl, part penguin, and part cat. Released in 1998, Furbies became the biggest toy fad of the new millennium; millions were sold.

Hampton, a lifelong tinkerer, got the idea for an interactive toy at the 1997 International Toy Fair, where he played with a Tamagotchi, a digital pet from Japan that existed only on a small LCD screen. The Tamagotchi's key feature: It would "die" if you didn't feed it. But Hampton sensed that kids wanted more than a screen to play with, so he created the Furby. When you turned the toy on, it spoke only "Furbish," a language invented by Hampton. But as you kept talking to it, it "learned" preprogrammed English words.

The Furby also recorded your voice and played it back at random…which is why it was banned by the National Security Agency. What's the use of a bug-proof room in a spy agency if there's a Furby sitting there, recording everything you're saying, ready to blab state secrets to the highest Russian bidder?

Toy Story

The Daisy company started selling Red Ryder BB guns in 1938, but never a "carbine-action, 200-shot Range Model air rifle with a compass in the stock and a thing which tells time!" Yet that's how *A Christmas Story* author Jean Shepherd remembered the rifle he had when he was a kid, so Daisy built one especially for the 1983 movie adaptation.

— ORIGINS —

Figure It Out

What board game was designed to pass
time during World War II air raids?

☞

Figure It Out

Colonel Mustard could answer this question, but he's otherwise occupied in the ballroom with a lead pipe. The game, of course, is Clue.

During World War II, England was under constant threat of German attacks. Hiding in cellars for hours during air raids was both terrifying and boring. So, looking for a way to pass the time, Anthony Pratt, a Birmingham, England, law clerk, created a mystery game called Murder. He later patented the game, which proved to be such a big hit that Parker Brothers released it in the United States as Clue. Waddingtons, a gaming company from Leeds, England, released it in the U.K. as Cluedo (a play on "clue" and *ludo*, Latin for "I play").

Pratt's original design called for 10 suspects, one of whom would be designated at random as the murder victim. The published board game featured six suspects and a perpetual murder victim (Mr. Black in England, Mr. Boddy in the U.S.); the publishers eliminated Mr. Brown, Mr. Gold, Miss Grey, and Mrs. Silver, and changed Nurse White and Colonel Yellow to Miss White and Colonel Mustard. They also streamlined the number of weapons, eliminating the bomb, syringe, poison, fireplace poker, Pratt's ax and—with a nod to the Irish—the *shillelagh* (a type of cudgel, or club). More than 100 million Clue games have sold.

—— ORIGINS ——

Dirty Young Man

At what magazine did Hugh Hefner
work while he raised the money
to start *Playboy*?

Mystery Meat

Which clothing line got its name
from a McDonald's billboard?

Dirty Young Man

Children's Activities. Hefner served as the magazine's circulation manager while he raised money to start his "sophisticated" men's magazine that would feature journalism, fiction, and nude women. Working title: *Stag Party.* (Hefner changed the name because another magazine—*Stag*—had threatened to sue.) Along with the cash he earned at *Children's Activities,* Hefner took out a loan to start *Playboy* (putting up his furniture as collateral) and borrowed the rest from his mom. In December 1953, working from his Chicago apartment, Hefner put all $8,000 into printing the first edition of *Playboy.* The first cover girl: Marilyn Monroe.

Mystery Meat

See if you can GUESS the answer. In 1977 four French brothers—Armand, Georges, Maurice, and Paul Marciano—moved to California to make their fortune in fashion. Their first label, Marilyn Designer Jeans, sold poorly despite the pop-culture reference, so the Marcianos started searching for a new name. While driving to work one day, Georges saw a McDonald's billboard. Displayed on it was a picture of a hamburger along with seven words, the first in all capital letters: "GUESS what's in the new Big Mac!" So they named their new line of jeans GUESS. (On a side note: Did McDonald's really think it was a good idea to make customers GUESS what's in their food?)

Screen Gem

What does the gaming term
"check" mean in Japanese?
And what does it have to do
with Chuck E. Cheese?

Screen Gem

The Japanese word for "check" is *atari*. It comes from a chess-like game called Go—one of the oldest board games in the world. An American computer engineer (and big fan of Go) named Nolan Bushnell decided to create a new generation of games.

In 1972 Bushnell and his partner Ted Dabney released the first commercially available coin-operated arcade game: Computer Space. (It was modeled after the pioneering 1962 video game Spacewar!, which had made its way to only a few college campuses.) But Computer Space didn't really catch on, either—the directions were too complicated. So Bushnell and Dabney came up with a table-tennis video game that didn't require directions. They called it PONG. "It's so simple," said Bushnell, "that any drunk in any bar could play it." And millions of drunks did just that. However, few of them could pronounce the company's name—Syzygy (although it might have been fun to hear them try). Besides, Syzygy (from the Latin for "conjunction") was also being used by a hippie candle-making company. Needing a new name for the company, Bushnell borrowed his favorite word from his favorite game...and Atari was born.

What does this have to do with Chuck E. Cheese, the pizza restaurant chain that features that creepy animatronic mouse band? In 1977 Bushnell invented that, too.

Low-Tar Education

What private school was named
after a brand of cigarettes?

Go West, Young Man

What sad news sent a 35-year-old man named
John B. Stetson on a journey that would
lead him to invent the cowboy hat?

Low-Tar Education

Waldorf Schools. In 1919 Emil Molt, the German manufacturer of the popular Waldorf cigarette brand, hired educational theorist Rudolf Steiner to create a new school for his factory workers' children. Today, there are 998 Waldorf Schools in 60 countries.

Interestingly, nearly everything named "Waldorf" has a common ancestor: The cigarettes were named after New York's Waldorf-Astoria Hotel, which in turn was named after its founder, William Waldorf Astor. Astor, in turn, got his middle name from his grandfather's birthplace—Waldorf, Germany.

Go West, Young Man

In 1865 Stetson was diagnosed with tuberculosis—his doctor gave him only six months to live. Longing to see the Wild West before he died, Stetson quit his father's hat business in New Jersey and took a train to the plains. He was awestruck by the open spaces and the rugged cowboys, but not by their hats. Stetson knew he could make something better than those tattered coonskin caps, sombreros, and sailor hats.

Six months later (and still not dead), Stetson moved to Philadelphia and opened a hat factory. His first product: the "Boss of the Plains," made out of beaver pelts. One cowboy raved, "It keeps the sun out of your eyes and off your neck. It's an umbrella, a bucket to water your horse, and a cup for yourself!" Despite costing more than most cowboys made in a month, millions of Bosses were sold every year in the late 1800s. Stetson lived until the ripe old age of 76.

Novelty Act

A white supremacist invented two
of the most popular mail-order toys
of the 20th century. Who was he,
and what were the toys?

Novelty Act

Harold von Braunhut. He invented and marketed dozens of mail-order toys, including two of the most famous: Amazing Sea-Monkeys and X-Ray Specs.

Born in Tennessee in 1926, his given name was Harold Braunhut. Raised Jewish in New York City, he later abandoned his upbringing and added "von" to his name to make it sound more German. In addition to holding 195 patents, von Braunhut once raced motorcycles under the name "The Green Hornet," and later managed novelty stage acts—including a guy who jumped from a 40-foot platform into a kiddie pool.

Always looking to make a quick buck, von Braunhut earned his fortune selling cheap toys to impressionable kids (like Uncle John) in the back of comic books. Most popular in the 1960s and '70s, and still sold today, Amazing Sea-Monkeys are actually brine shrimp. But X-Ray Specs really do let you see through bones and clothes! Actually, they don't—they simply diffract light, causing the viewer to see a sort of aura around the object. Von Braunhut's toys were junk, but his marketing skills were priceless. "So eager to please, they can even be trained!" he boasted on the Amazing Sea-Monkeys box.

For years, a rumor circulated that von Braunhut was a white supremacist. Turns out, it's true: He sent a portion of his profits to the Aryan Nations organization, and was often quoted as saying, "Hitler wasn't a bad guy. He just received bad press."

Check Marks the Spot

Graphic designer Carolyn Davidson's
second-most famous design is for the
wallpaper in a Yakima, Washington,
motel. What's her most famous design?

☞

Check Marks the Spot

The Nike Swoosh. In 1971 the young design student was doodling in her accounting class at Oregon's Portland State University. Impressed by her drawing skills, Davidson's professor asked her if she could put together a few ideas for a symbol to be printed on his new line of running shoes.

That professor was Phil Knight. Seven years earlier, he and track-and-field coach Bill Bowerman had started an athletic shoe distribution company called Blue Ribbon Sports. Now they wanted to create a new kind of running shoe that could compete with the German brands adidas and Puma.

Davidson came up with a few ideas for the symbol. Knight wasn't that impressed with any of them, but he chose one that resembled a curvy check mark. "I don't love it," Knight said, "but it will grow on me." (He was right.) How much did Davidson charge him for the design? $35. Knight soon renamed the company after Nike, the Greek goddess of victory, who sat by Zeus's side as he presided over the Olympics. Within a few years, Nike was among the premiere athletic shoe companies in the world, and the Swoosh has since become one of the most recognizable symbols.

In 1983 Knight gave Davidson a thank-you gift: 500 shares of Nike stock worth more than $1 million. At last report, she still hasn't cashed them in, but is retired and happily volunteering her time at the Ronald McDonald House in Portland, Oregon. "I have a blessed life," she said. "And there's so much hurt in the world, I just thought I should give back."

BUSY BODIES

Do you have any idea how many things are happening inside you right now—churning, pumping, flowing, absorbing? It's amazing…and at the same time, it's kind of gross. Here are some questions about what makes us tick.

Just Like Tiny Drunkards

Why do toddlers wobble?

☞

Some Nerve

What's the largest unprotected nerve in your body?

☞

Just Like Tiny Drunkards

You'd wobble too if your head were roughly a quarter
the weight of the rest of your body. By the time you're
fully grown, your head will weigh only about one-
eighth as much as the rest of your body, and therefore
be a lot easier to hold up…unless you happen to have
an abnormally large head, like Uncle John, who still
sometimes wobbles when he walks.

Some Nerve

The *ulnar nerve* is the medical term for the funny
bone, which is neither bone nor funny, although you
may find it "humerus" to see your friend writhe in
agony after a bump to the elbow.

Why is it so agonizing? It's a case of poor place-
ment. The ulnar is one of the three main nerves that
run from the collarbone to the hand. This particular
nerve provides sensation in the pinky and the adja-
cent half of the ring finger. It also happens to be unprotected, meaning that there's very little bone or
muscle tissue to shield it from trauma. Result: It takes
only a slight tap in just the right spot near the elbow
to send your entire arm into a tingling frenzy. Interestingly, the temporary discomfort is very similar to the
permanent discomfort experienced by sufferers of
carpal tunnel syndrome, which affects the ulnar nerve
where it passes through the base of the hand.

No, It's Not the Brain

Which mostly useless body part
is named after the beak of a bird?

☞

No, It's Not the Brain

The *coccyx*, also known as your tailbone. The word comes from an ancient Greek word for "cuckoo bird" because the bone looks like the bird's beak.

It's a strange fusion of bones, the coccyx. Your spine is probably the most important sets of bones in your body (it holds up your head, after all), but at the base of the spine, right above your bottom, the fusion of bones that makes up your coccyx doesn't really do much for stability (except for when you're sitting). It's not entirely useless, though—the coccyx connects several important muscles and ligaments.

In most mammals, the coccyx is *very* important: That's where the tail begins—hence its other name, the *tailbone*. In humans and some other primates, the coccyx is nearly identical to that of other mammals; there's just no tail. So could we conceivably grow tails? Yes, except that the gene that instructs a tail to grow is not turned on. What would it take to turn on that gene? A genetic mutation—which could possibly lead to a small group of isolated humans growing tails.

That reminds us of one of the weirdest quotations of all time. Actor Christopher Walken once opined: "How great it would be if actors had tails! Because a tail is so expressive. On a cat you can tell everything. You can tell if they're annoyed. You can tell whether they're scared. I wish I had a tail."

Wrap Stars

What's the main ingredient in
the old-fashioned cure-all
known as "Mummy Powder"?

The Host with the Most

How many organisms are living
on and inside you right now?

Wrap Stars

Mummies…as in, the remains of dead people. By the 12th century, many doctors in Europe and Asia were grinding mummies into powder and using it as medicine. Not unlike other quack remedies, mummy powder was prescribed to heal all sorts of ailments: epilepsy, migraines, nausea, sore throat, fractures, and even paralysis. Used as a tea or a poultice, it remained popular through the 1800s (even Abraham Lincoln supposedly drank it). There are, however, no known healing properties of mummy powder, and the fad died out at the end of the 19th century. Unfortunately for archaeologists, the practice of grinding the remains into powder destroyed several thousand mummies—along with whatever information they could have provided about how ancient people lived and died.

The Host with the Most

As many as two quadrillion bacteria microbes. We are made up of cells, approximately 100 trillion of them. Moving within, on, under, and between those cells are an incredible number of uninvited guests. In fact, for every one cell in the human body, there are somewhere in the neighborhood of 10 to 20 times as many microbes, both healthy and unhealthy. That totals roughly 2,000,000,000,000,000 bacteria, concentrated in the places where microbial communities prosper: the nose, mouth, skin, digestive tract—and in females, the urogenital tract. Your skin alone is host to upwards of 500 different species of bacteria.

Baby Got Back

When you were a baby, what did you
have 100 more of than you do now?

He Had a Gut Feeling

Why did Australian doctor
Barry Marshall's experiments
give him an ulcer?

☞

Baby Got Back

Bones. You were born with around 350 of them. Over time, many of the bones—mostly in your spine—fused together into single, larger bones, reducing the number by nearly a third to 206 bones in an average adult. That doesn't mean that you definitely have 206 bones. Not everyone's baby bones all fuse together, so you may actually have a few more.

He Had a Gut Feeling

Dr. Marshall gave himself the ulcer…on purpose. Until the 1980s, the prevailing notion was that ulcers are caused by stress. Marshall believed otherwise. He hypothesized that ulcers are caused by corkscrew-shaped bacteria known as *Helicobacter pylori*. When he announced his theory in 1982, the medical community laughed at him. Every doctor worth his diploma knew that bacteria can't survive in stomach acid. Marshall was convinced they could but was having trouble proving that to his peers. Why? The usual test subjects—pigs and rats—aren't affected by *H. pylori*. So Marshall cooked up a batch of the bacteria and drank it himself. Result: He got a raging ulcer, which proved his theory and changed the way ulcers are treated.

Footnote: Back in 1899, a Polish doctor named Walery Jaworski discovered *H. pylori* and even suggested that it might cause some stomach ills. However, his theory remained unknown outside of Poland until Marshall's discovery.

Mover

What are the three parts
of the small intestine?

Floater

The hip bone may be connected to the thigh
bone, but there's one bone that's not connected
to any other bone. Do you know what it is?
(A forensic investigator sure does.)

Pumper

How many gallons of blood will
your heart pump today?

Mover

The *duodenum, jejunum,* and *ileum* make up the small intestine, which is about 18 feet long and an inch in diameter. After leaving the stomach, partially digested food enters the C-shaped duodenum, which is about a foot long. Next, it goes into the jejunum and then to the ileum, both of which twist and turn upon themselves. The inner linings of these two sections contain tiny finger-like bumps called *villi*; their job is to absorb nutrients into the bloodstream. What's left of your meal then goes to the large intestine. Although it's only five feet long, it's much wider—about three inches in diameter (which is why it's referred to as "large"). The entire journey takes several hours…and ends with a flush.

Floater

It's the *hyoid bone*, and it's unique in that no other bone touches it. Located in the neck just above the larynx, the hyoid anchors the tongue muscles. This bone is well known to forensic investigators: If a deceased person's hyoid is broken, it almost always means that the cause of death was strangulation.

Pumper

About 2,000 gallons, if you're average. The heart has to pump that much because most adults have about 60,000 miles of blood vessels through which the blood must continually flow. How far is 60,000 miles? More than two trips around the equator.

Workplace Hazards

Inflamed tendons, dental injuries, erythema, scaling, cyst formation, scarring, and inflammatory pustules. These types of maladies are common among members of what profession?

☞

Workplace Hazards

Were you thinking football players? Cops? Deep-sea fishermen? How about pro wrestlers? Wrong. The answer is classical musicians, who are prone to painful, sometimes career-ending, afflictions similar to those suffered by athletes. This isn't surprising, considering that professional musicians perform repetitive motions for as many as six hours every day—which is how much you have to practice to get that good.

Case in point: A cellist's left hand, playing just the last movement of Mahler's Fifth Symphony, changes position on the strings roughly 6,400 times. Other examples of common injuries and maladies suffered by classical musicians:

• Violinists can develop skin cysts and pustules on their necks. (It's called "fiddler's neck.")

• String players are also especially prone to chronic pain in their shoulders, arms, and neck.

• Keyboard and woodwind players can suffer from wrist injuries to the point of becoming unable to use silverware or turn doorknobs.

• Pressure from a brass instrument's mouthpiece can cause dental, lip, and facial nerve damage.

• And no matter where the musician sits in an orchestra, he or she will most likely be exposed to more than enough loud noises to cause at least some hearing loss. A study of classical musicians by a group of Finnish researchers reported that 15 percent of the musicians suffered from permanent tinnitus—a constant ringing in the ears. In contrast, that condition only affects 2 percent of the general population.

Papers, Please

If your body were a country, which organ
would be considered the customs agent?

Perchance to Dream

Nearly everyone experiences typical
REM sleep, except for one specific
group of people. Who are they?

Papers, Please

Just like a customs agent who checks everything that enters a country, your liver checks the stuff that enters your body. That's not all it does: The liver performs an estimated 500 different functions. Located just behind your rib cage, it's is responsible for dealing with 99 percent of the chemicals you ingest, and it even manufactures chemicals of its own. Your liver also assists in digestion by converting most of the vitamins, carbohydrates, protein, and fat that you ingest into the nutrients your body needs. And as if that weren't enough, it also works to keep all the toxins you ingest from spreading throughout your body, either by destroying them or sending them to the toilet.

Perchance to Dream

The only people who don't experience typical REM sleep are people who were blind from birth. Short for "Rapid Eye Movement," REM is what your eyes do when you dream—basically, they're "looking around" at images created by your brain. That doesn't mean that blind people don't dream—just that they don't see anything. Instead, they smell, touch, and hear things in their dreams, just as they do in life. Sighted people who become blind will still "see" in their dreams, although most report that as the years go by, sight in dreams diminishes and is gradually replaced by other senses.

—— BUSY BODIES ——

Patriotic Discharge

What smelly affliction did
Benjamin Franklin believe could
be cured by ingesting turpentine?

The Riddler

I am a part of your body whose job
it is to receive something that enters
you and then convert it into something
else. Only then will you know what
that thing is. I was fully grown when
you were only two. What am I?

Patriotic Discharge

Franklin was attempting to cure smelly asparagus pee. "A few stems of asparagus," he wrote, "shall give our urine a disagreeable odor; a pill of turpentine no bigger than a pea shall bestow upon it the pleasing smell of violets." Franklin was right about the odor—eating asparagus does cause the body to produce sulfur compounds that are then released in urine. Not everyone can detect it, but to those who can (including, apparently, Franklin) the smell can be quite offensive. (Warning: Uncle John doesn't recommend taking the bizarre medical advice of Benjamin Franklin or any other forefather.)

The Riddler

The retinas. Like the sensor in a camera, the retinas' job is to convert light waves that enter your eyes into electrical impulses. The impulses are then sent to your brain, where they're converted into visual images.

All mammalian eyes grow to full size faster than most of the rest of the body (which is why young mammals all look so cute—it's those "big" eyes). The retinas, located in the back of the eyeballs, are the first to mature; the rest of the eyes become fully grown by puberty. In contrast, the brain doesn't become fully mature until the late 30s to early 40s. (Or, in the case of some people we know, never.)

Anyone for Ping-Pong?

If you force your eyes to stay open
when you sneeze, how far, in feet, will
your eyeballs fly out of your head?

Lose Weight the
Uncle John Way!

By the time you reach 70 years old, you will
have lost more than 100 pounds of what?

Anyone for Ping-Pong?

As cool as that would be to witness, nobody's eyes have ever popped out of their sockets during an open-eye sneeze. The pressure of a sneeze is confined to your nasal passages, not your eyes. So why do you close your eyes when you sneeze? Like the sneeze itself—a reaction to rid the nasal passages of irritants—closing your eyes is an involuntary reflex.

But unlike sneezing, it's still a medical mystery as to exactly why this eye-closing reflex occurs. The two prevailing theories: 1) Closing the eyes keeps nasty sneeze projectiles from spraying into the eyes and then reentering the body; and 2) sneezing forces air backward from the nose through the tear ducts, creating a puff of air that causes the eyes to close.

Although some people claim to have trained themselves to sneeze with their eyes open, for most of us, if we try to force our eyes to stay open, the sneeze reflex simply diminishes.

Lose Weight the Uncle John Way!

Dead skin cells. You shed them at a rate of about 600,000 per hour. If you were somehow able to collect all of this debris, you'd have well over one pound per year and more than 100 pounds by the time you were 70. (Of course, that's impossible. Most dead skin cells just float away. You would have to vacuum yourself almost constantly.)

Cheese Factory

Eight have three bones.
Two have two bones.
What are they?

Totally Worth It

You've come down with a severe case
of *sphenopalatine ganglioneuralgia*.
It's unbearable! What did you do
to cause yourself so much pain?

Cheese Factory

Toes. Your big toe, called your *hallux*, has only two bones—the *proximal* and *distal phalanges*. All your other toes each have three bones: the *proximal*, *middle*, and *distal phalanges* (singularly called a *phalanx*). The hallux is your main weight-bearing toe; the other little piggies help you maintain balance.

Totally Worth It

You ate that bowl of ice cream *way* too fast. Now you've got a nasty ice-cream headache, otherwise known as a "brain freeze" or, as some like to call it, "Iceburger's Syndrome." Physicians, however, call it *sphenopalatine ganglioneuralgia*...which means "pain in the sphenopalatine ganglion"—a cluster of nerve cells located just above the roof of your mouth. So why does this happen? When you consume something cold, this nerve cluster alerts your brain that the temperature inside your head is falling drastically. Your brain tries to warm up the affected area by sending in a rush of blood. The blood vessels first constrict and then dilate, and because the sphenopalatine ganglion lies close to other nerves, the increased blood flow puts pressure on them as well, causing acute but temporary pain to your face and forehead.

The moral: Slow down. (Like Mrs. Uncle John always says, "Relax. No one is going to take away your ice cream.")

—— BUSY BODIES ——

Turn Off Your Blinkers

In the "Flora and Fauna" chapter, we asked how long a cockroach could live without its head. According to an infamous French experiment, how long can a decapitated human head maintain consciousness?

☞

Turn Off Your Blinkers

Antoine Lavoisier (1743–94), a French nobleman and scientist, is considered the "father of modern chemistry." He's also known for the grisly experiment—his last—that provides the answer to this question.

First, some background: In his distinguished career, Lavoisier coined the terms *oxygen* and *hydrogen*, helped create the metric system, and was the first person to state the law of conservation of mass, which says, "Although matter may change its form or shape, its mass always remains the same." Despite his discoveries, Lavoisier's "elitist scientific ways" branded him as an enemy of the people during the French Revolution. Said the judge at his trial, "The Republic needs neither scientists nor chemists; the course of justice cannot be delayed."

Verdict: Lavoisier was sentenced to death by the guillotine. Ever the scientist, he asked an associate to stand nearby during the execution. "Watch my eyes after the blade comes down," he instructed. "I will continue blinking as long as I retain consciousness." His friend did as he was told, watch in hand.

The time elapsed between the drop of the blade and Lavoisier's last blink: 15 seconds. (That didn't really prove anything, except that humans can still exhibit involuntary muscle movements after they die.)

Headnote: A year later, French rulers realized they acted a bit overzealously…and exonerated Lavoisier posthumously.

Pay It No Mind

When something painful happens to you, it is your brain that tells you that you're hurting. Why is that odd?

Iron Chef

What can be made from these ingredients: bacteria (both dead and dying), mucus, cellulose, cholesterol, phosphates, dead cells, bilirubin, and water?

Pay It No Mind

It's kind of ironic, but the brain—which informs you when something hurts—cannot actually sense pain when the brain itself is injured. Why? There are no nerve endings up there. So if you stub your toe, you'll scream, but if you stick an ice pick into your brain, you won't feel a thing. (That's not to say you won't experience any odd side effects, or that the skin covering your skull won't hurt, but at least your brain will refrain from feeling pain.)

Iron Chef

Poop. It's actually three-quarters water, unless you happen to have diarrhea, in which case it's almost all water. And if you're constipated, the poop stays inside you too long and a lot of the water is extracted, which results in dry, painful bowel movements. As to the other ingredients: The phosphates are inorganic salts which, along with cholesterol, you didn't digest. The mucus comes from your intestinal walls. The dead and dying bacteria produce sulfur- or nitrogen-rich organic compounds such as *indole*, *skatole*, and *mercaptans*, as well as *hydrogen sulfide*. (That's what makes poop smell.) *Bilirubin* is a pigment that results from the breakdown of red blood cells. (That's what makes poop brown.) Finally, the cellulose is the fiber that binds it all together. It also gives your poop traction as it moves through your intestines. Sure, it's gross—but at least it's outside of you now. Good riddance!

PUBLIC LIVES

*In this chapter, we quiz you about movers
and shakers both famous and obscure.*

Sign of Genius

How much did Albert Einstein charge
for his autograph—and who was the
only celebrity who got it for free?

Funny Lady

Who was the first female game-show
host to win an Emmy award?

Sign of Genius

The greatest thinker of the 20th century charged $1 per autograph, which, in the 1950s, was roughly the equivalent of $10. Einstein did this for two reasons: 1) It reduced the number of people who bothered him for an autograph (for a scientist, he was very famous), and 2) it also helped the charities to which he donated the money. There was, however, one notable exception: Einstein gave a free autograph to one of his heroes, silent film star Charlie Chaplin. The comedic genius accepted the gift humbly, telling the physics genius, "People cheer me because they all understand me, and they cheer you because nobody understands you."

Funny Lady

Betty White. A TV star since the 1950s, she hosted the 1983 NBC daytime game show *Just Men!* It featured two female contestants who asked yes-or-no questions to seven male celebrities for a chance to win a convertible Ford Mustang. Among the celebrities: Fred Willard, Hervé Villechaize (Tattoo from *Fantasy Island*), and *Wheel of Fortune's* Pat Sajak, who was just starting out. Despite the fact that the show lasted only 13 weeks, White won the 1983 Emmy for Best Daytime Host.

White won her first Emmy in 1951 for her starring role in the sitcom *Life With Elizabeth*. In 2010 she won her seventh Emmy for hosting *Saturday Night Live*.

Foresight

Where can you see Louis
Armstrong's famous trumpet?

Persona Non Grata

Philip Cohen was a vaudeville performer
who went by the name Phil Roy. His son,
Jacob, followed in his father's footsteps,
performing under the name Jack Roy,
but later changed it to what?

Foresight

You can't, but maybe your grandchildren can. That's because in the year 2000, the U.S. National Archives placed Satchmo's trumpet into the Millennium Time Capsule, which won't be opened until 2100—giving our descendants a chance to see a few 20th-century artifacts, including (besides the trumpet) a transistor, a piece of the Berlin Wall, and a film showing Neil Armstrong's moonwalk.

Persona Non Grata

Rodney Dangerfield. Born in 1921 as Jacob Cohen, he spent years trying to break into the comedy business using the name Jack Roy, but met with failure after failure (because he "lacked a persona," as he put it). Cohen eventually gave up show business and sold aluminum siding to support his family. But he just couldn't give up on his dream.

At the age of 45, he returned to the stage, performing his self-deprecating stand-up act in small clubs… and in 1967 landed a spot on *The Ed Sullivan Show*. His act was a hit, but he wanted to distance himself from his previous (failed) career, so he changed his name to Rodney Dangerfield. Where'd he get that name? A nightclub owner gave it to him. Where did the club owner get it from? He heard Ricky Nelson use it on *The Adventures of Ozzie and Harriet*. Where did Nelson get it from? He heard it on the radio: The name of a comical cowboy character on Jack Benny's radio show in 1941 was…Rodney Dangerfield.

Special Delivery

American actor Andy Garcia (*Ocean's Eleven*,
The Godfather Part III) was born with
what unusual birth defect?

Macabre Matinee

What movie was playing in the theater
that Lee Harvey Oswald ran into
after (allegedly) shooting JFK?

Special Delivery

Garcia was not born alone. Immediately after his birth, doctors noticed a softball-sized growth on his left shoulder. It turned out to be an underdeveloped, parasitic twin that had stopped growing early in gestation…and lived off of baby Andy in the womb. The doctors immediately removed the conjoined twin, whereupon it died. (Garcia still has a scar on his shoulder.) After he became a famous actor, his sibling became a running joke on *The Howard Stern Show*— Stern mused that the twin was "the one who got all the personality."

Macabre Matinee

War Is Hell, a Korean War drama (in black-and-white) directed by Burt Topper and starring Tony Russel. It was the first half of a double feature (the other film was called *Cry of Battle*) playing at the Texas Theater in Dallas on November 22, 1963. A few blocks away, President Kennedy's motorcade was traveling down Elm Street; the President was shot while riding in the back of his convertible (a Lincoln).

Shortly after the movie started, Oswald ran into the theater without paying the 90-cent admission fee. The manager called the police. While a blaze of gunfire was exploding on the screen, Oswald was captured and taken into custody. Interestingly, the film had been delayed from release for three years because of its alleged anti-American sentiments.

Coming Attractions

What future Oscar-winning actress
was fifth-billed under Justine Bateman,
Britta Phillips, and two others as a
sex-crazed bass player in the 1988
girl-rocker movie *Satisfaction*?
Who got second billing
in that film?

☞

Coming Attractions

Julia Roberts. Her big-screen debut came as Daryle, the sex-crazed bass player in this well-publicized but poorly reviewed movie about a girl band trying to make it big. Directed by Joan Freeman (her second and final feature film—her first was 1985's *Streetwalkin'*), *Satisfaction* was intended to launch the film career of TV star Bateman (Mallory on *Family Ties*). But the movie and Bateman's feature-film career flopped. (Don't cry for her—she's had a successful run as a TV actor and fashion designer.)

Julia Roberts, who was only 20 when *Satisfaction* was filmed, went on to superstardom two years later after she took a role that several better-known, A-list actresses—including Meg Ryan, Michelle Pfeiffer, and Daryl Hannah—turned down: the hooker with a heart in 1990's *Pretty Woman*. Roberts later won a Best Actress Oscar for her starring role in the 2000 legal drama *Erin Brockovich*.

Second-billed in *Satisfaction:* Liam Neeson. He played a nightclub owner and Bateman's love interest. The Irish actor claims he only took the role because he'd just completed a much darker film called *Suspect* in which he played a deaf mute accused of murder. After that, Neeson reportedly wanted to spend some time in the sun and be around pretty girls. He claims he's never actually seen *Satisfaction*…and never plans to.

A Sack to Remember

Who owns Davy Crockett's pouch?

☞

All Together Now

Only three music artists have sold more than 100 million albums twice—first as part of a band, and then again as a solo act. Two of them are Michael Jackson and Paul McCartney. Who is the third?

☞

Who Said No

Who begged Pete Townshend to let him take over as drummer of the Who after Keith Moon died?

A Sack to Remember

Phil Collins. The British rocker and former Genesis drummer is obsessed with the Alamo; according to some accounts, he believes he was actually there in a past life. Collins owns one of the world's most extensive collections of Alamo memorabilia, including the pouch in which Davy Crockett kept his musket balls. Several tabloids have reported that a psychic once told the singer he's the reincarnation of messenger John W. Smith, who played a part in the 1836 battle for Texas independence. But Collins's lifelong fascination with the Alamo is more than just tabloid fodder; he's a respected Alamo historian who tours Texas giving lectures on the subject.

All Together Now

Phil Collins. He sold 159 million albums as a member of Genesis, and another 155 million albums as a solo act. He's also won seven Grammy awards and an Academy Award for the song "You'll Be in My Heart" from Disney's *Tarzan*.

Who Said No

Phil Collins. He was a big fan of the Who (more than Genesis, it turned out). In the mid-1970s, Collins told Who frontman Pete Townshend, "If you ever need a drummer, I'm there. I'll leave Genesis in a moment." After Moon died of a drug overdose in 1978, Collins asked again. Townshend turned him down and chose former Small Faces drummer Kenney Jones instead.

A Scar Is Born

How did Tina Fey get her scar?

☞

The Blue Lagoon? Really?

What heavyweight movie star was originally
slated to star in *The Blue Lagoon* (1980),
Arthur (1981), *Night Shift* (1982),
and *Three Amigos* (1986)?

☞

A Scar Is Born

If you didn't know that Tina Fey has a scar on her face, it's because the star of TV's *30 Rock* has spent most of her on-screen career trying to hide it—either with makeup or by making sure she's filmed from her right side only. She got the scar when she was five years old. Fey was playing in her front yard in Upper Darby, Pennsylvania, when a stranger walked up and cut the left side of her face with a knife. Then he ran away. At first, Fey thought it was a red pen mark. It wasn't. Little else is known about the incident—Fey herself never talks about it in public. (Her husband, Jeff Richmond, however, spilled the beans to *Vanity Fair* in 2008.)

The Blue Lagoon? Really?

John Belushi. His death by drug overdose in 1982 at the age of 33 sent shock waves throughout the entertainment industry that lasted for years. He was cast in or attached to a dozen film roles, so all the projects had to be either scrapped or postponed after his sudden demise. The biggest movie: *Ghostbusters*, in which Belushi was scheduled to play the lead. (The part ultimately went to Bill Murray, but Richard Pryor was also considered.) And yes, before he died, Belushi was considered for the lead role in *The Blue Lagoon*, but the film's producers realized that the serious tone they were looking for might be jeopardized by the portly Belushi swimming around in a loincloth with Brooke Shields.

Quack-Up

What famous 20th-century explorer's last name translates to "wild duck" in English?

☞

Upstairs, Downstairs

Who is the tallest actor to ever win an Academy Award? Who is the shortest?

☞

What a Hunk

In 1940 the Division of Fine Arts at the University of Southern California selected a male model (a student who posed for sculptors) as having the "most nearly perfect male figure." Who was this dashing young man?

☞

Quack-Up

Yuri Gagarin—the Russian cosmonaut, who, on April 12, 1961, became the first human being to go into space. About an hour and a half after Gagarin blasted off on his one-orbit trip around Earth, his *Vostok* capsule re-entered the atmosphere. He ejected and then parachuted down onto a field in a remote region of southern Russia, where a farmer and her daughter saw the strange man in an orange jumpsuit fall out of the sky. As they started to run away, Gagarin shouted, "I am a friend, comrades, a friend!"

The girl turned around and asked, "Can it be that you have come from outer space?"

"As a matter of fact, I have!" Gagarin replied. Then he asked to use a phone so he could call Moscow and get someone to come out and pick him up.

Upstairs, Downstairs

Six-foot-five-inch Tim Robbins is the tallest. He won the Best Supporting Actor Oscar for the 2003 drama *Mystic River*. Measuring 3'5", the shortest Oscar winner was Shirley Temple, who won a special Academy Award in 1934 at the age of six. Temple later went into politics, serving as a foreign ambassador for Presidents Nixon, Ford, Carter, and the first Bush.

What a Hunk

That hunky student was Ronald Reagan, who went on to costar with a chimpanzee in *Bedtime for Bonzo*.

Trendsetter

1920s silent film star Mae Murray
accidentally dropped something…
and started a national craze.
What did she drop?

☞

Trendsetter

Her doughnut. Murray was an early Hollywood sex symbol known as "the girl with the bee-stung lips." She's also known as the first person to dunk a doughnut into a cup of coffee. It happened one day in 1925. Murray, who'd recently starred in *The Merry Widow*, was eating in a New York City deli when she accidentally dropped her doughnut into her cup of joe. A hush fell over the table. Murray wasn't fazed, though. Surprising everyone, she extracted the soggy pastry and *actually took a bite out of it*! Then she raved about how delicious it was.

Word of Murray's happy accident quickly spread throughout the entertainment community. Over the next few years, anybody who was anybody was dunking their doughnuts. Groucho Marx dunked his in *Duck Soup*. Clark Gable taught Claudette Colbert how to dunk hers in *It Happened One Night*. There was even a "National Dunking Association" with such esteemed members as Red Skelton, Jimmy Durante, Pearl Buck, and a young comedian named Johnny Carson. Dunking doughnuts became such a part of popular culture that it inspired the fast-food chain, Dunkin' Donuts, which opened its doors in Quincy, Massachusetts, in 1950.

Whatever happened to Mae Murray? She'd probably be more popular today had she not angered movie mogul Louis B. Mayer by quitting MGM in 1927. He had her blacklisted from the other studios, and she appeared in only three more films. (Doughnuts, however, appear in millions of coffee cups every day.)

DOWN THE HATCH

*Now we tempt your palate with a few culinary delights,
along with a few culinary disasters you wouldn't feed
your dog. First up—two questions about beer.*

Pewter to the People

Why do German beer steins
come with hinged lids?

Measure for Measure

How many pints in a firkin?

Pewter to the People

To keep the flies out. In the Middle Ages, Germany experienced several massive fly swarms at the same time Europe was suffering from the "Black Death," in which millions of people were killed by the bubonic plague. Believing the flies were responsible for the disease, German rulers passed a law that all food and drink containers be fitted with a hinged lid. Although the law didn't stop the plague—which was actually caused by fleas that hopped from rats to humans—it did mark the beginning of a more sanitary age in Europe. Most food and beverage containers lost their lids after the plague subsided, but lidded German beer steins remained in vogue for three more centuries... and still exist today.

Measure for Measure

In merry old England, a *firkin* was a unit of measurement used by brewers. Whenever someone was going to throw a big party, they had to first pick up a firkin or two.

The word itself derives from the Middle Dutch word *vierdekijn*, or "fourth." Hence, a firkin is equal to one quarter of a barrel, or 72 pints of beer. But wait, there's more: A firkin is equal to nine imperial gallons (English) as well as half of a *kilderkid* (Old English), about 41 liters (metric), and roughly half a keg (American). Pretty firkin confusing, isn't it?

A Safari in Your Mouth

Frog legs supposedly taste like chicken.
There are several other "exotic food
tastes like…" comparisons, such as
lion and boa constrictor taste like _____;
armadillo, wombat, beaver,
and human taste like _____;
zebra and hippo taste like _____;
and wasp larvae taste like _____.

☞

Chunky Style

How many insect parts and rat hairs does
the FDA allow in a jar of peanut butter?
And why do they allow any of these
gross things in your food?

A Safari in Your Mouth

Exotic-food buffs claim that lion and boa constrictor meat tastes like veal. Armadillo—called "Hoover hog" by the people who ate it to survive during the Great Depression (when Herbert Hoover was president)—is said to taste like pork. Also tasting like pork: wombats, beavers, and people. Zebra and hippo meat are often compared to beef. In both taste and texture, eating wasp larvae is supposedly a lot like eating scrambled eggs.

Chunky Style

The U.S. Food and Drug Administration allows for an average of "30 or more insect fragments and one or more rodent hairs per 100 grams of peanut butter." Why not ban them outright? The FDA considers these beastly additives to be a natural byproduct of making processed foods. The government agency's booklet "Food Defect Action Levels" explains, "It is economically impractical to grow, harvest, or process raw products that are totally free of non-hazardous, naturally occurring, unavoidable defects." What, then, is your actual insect and rodent-hair intake? Recent studies have reported that Americans consume about a pound of them per year. Good news: According to entomologists, the protein from the bugs is actually healthier than the pesticides used to keep them out. The rat hairs, however, have no health benefit…but they don't harm you, either.

—— DOWN THE HATCH ——

Sweet Explorer

On his two-year trip to the South Pole
in the 1930s, Admiral Robert Byrd
carried 2.5 tons of what candy?
On which holiday are you most
likely to see these candies?

☞

Carnivore's Dream

In what single meal might you eat a camel, lion,
monkey, hippopotamus, rhinoceros, zebra,
bison, gorilla, cougar, elephant, giraffe,
hyena, kangaroo, seal, sheep, tiger,
bear, polar bear, and koala?

☞

Sweet Explorer

Necco Wafers. Rear Admiral Byrd was a World War I fighter pilot who later became the U.S. Navy's most trusted explorer, leading expeditions to both poles. For his journey to Antarctica, Byrd allotted a daily ration of one pack of Neccos per crew member. Why Necco Wafers? First, because they were cheap; second, because they were an efficient way of adding needed calories to his crew's diet. Plus, the chalky wafers weren't affected by extremes of heat and cold and didn't spoil over long periods of time. It was these same characteristics that prompted the U.S. military to requisition the bulk of Necco's production runs during World War II.

On what holiday are you most likely to be given a Necco Wafer? Valentine's Day. Every February, Necco's parent company, the New England Confectionery Company, sells about eight billion heart-shaped Necco Wafers stamped with loving messages, such as "Be mine" and "U R A 10." Called "Sweethearts," they've been a Valentine's Day tradition for more than a century.

Carnivore's Dream

In a box of Barnum's Animals, commonly referred to as animal crackers. Invented in England in the 1800s, they've been distributed in the U.S. by Nabisco since 1902. The two most recent additions—both in the 21st century—are the koala and the polar bear.

Food Fight

What food do you blow up
and then drown?

Morning Tropic Thunder

Worldwide, coffee is grown in more than
50 countries, including the United
States. How many U.S. states
grow coffee commercially?

Food Fight

Popcorn. This staple snack is made from dried corn kernels. There's water on the inside, but it's sealed in. When the kernels are heated, that water turns to steam. The pressure builds...and builds...and builds...and then—BOOM! The hard shell explodes and propels the now-softened internal starch outward, which immediately hardens as the superheated water evaporates. Then all you have to do is throw the popcorn into a bowl and drown it in butter.

Morning Tropic Thunder

Two. Hawaii used to be the only U.S. state that grew coffee, but recently, small-scale organic coffee growers have popped up in the coastal areas near Santa Barbara, California. (It's also grown in Puerto Rico, but that's not a state...yet.) Why so few? Although coffee is the second most traded product in the world (petroleum is the first), the ideal climate conditions for growing it are rare. The small evergreen tree that produces coffee beans—which are actually the bitter pit of the tree's fruit—can grow only in regions that have a cool, mostly dry tropical winter, interrupted occasionally by rains that increase in frequency as the crop matures. Largest coffee grower: Brazil, responsible for 30 percent of the world's output.

Footnote: Instant coffee was invented by George Washington. Not the president, but George Constant Louis Washington, a Belgian-born American inventor who lived in Guatemala in the early 1900s.

— DOWN THE HATCH —

Sweet Scholarship

Which private school for children
is widely considered to be one of the
wealthiest in the world? Two hints:
1) It's in Pennsylvania.
2) You're in the food category.

☞

Sweet Scholarship

The Milton Hershey School, located in Hershey,
Pennsylvania. It owns 56 percent of the chocolate
company's stock, with assets worth nearly $6 billion,
making it one of the richest schools in the world.
Serving nearly 2,000 low-income students, the K–12
institution is located on the same land as the Hershey
family farm, where Milton Snavely Hershey was born
in 1857. In the 1860s, his parents moved so often that
he'd attended seven schools by the time he reached
the fourth grade…and he never made it to the fifth
grade. (Good thing that candy-making apprenticeship
paid off.)

In the early 1900s, Hershey, by then a millionaire,
and his wife, Kitty, tried to start a family, but Kitty was
unable to bear children. The Hersheys decided that if
they couldn't have their own family, they'd help children who didn't have families—or, like Milton, were
too poor to attend school. So in 1909 the couple opened
the Hershey Industrial School, a boarding academy for
"poor, healthy, white, male orphans between the ages
of 8 and 18." After Kitty died in 1915, Hershey
decided to keep her legacy alive by transferring the
majority of his assets, including control of the company, into the school's trust fund. Now known as the
Milton Hershey School, it's changed with the times,
allowing children of color (1968) and girls (1977).
And because it's located on the site of the family
farm, until 1989 milking cows was part of the curriculum. Of course, chocolate milk is still served in the
cafeteria.

The More, the Berrier

Who invented the loganberry,
the youngberry, and the boysenberry?
And which of these berries later
inspired a famous amusement park?

The More, the Berrier

Logan, Young, and Boysen.

• In 1883 James Harvey Logan of Santa Cruz, California, attempted to cross-breed two blackberry varieties, but they were planted too close to a vintage raspberry, which added its pollen to the mix. Of the 50 seeds Logan planted from this accidental union, one produced a plant with berries tasty enough that he reproduced the results, thus creating the loganberry.

• Byrnes M. Young, a Louisiana businessman who dabbled in horticulture on the side, crossed a blackberry with a dewberry (a cousin of the blackberry) in 1905 and got the youngberry.

• In 1923 horticulturist Rudolf Boysen crossed several varieties of blackberries, raspberries, and loganberries near Napa, California. His berries didn't sell well, so he gave up and moved south to Orange County.

Another California grower—Walter Knott—had heard about Boysen's unusual berries, so he went to the old fields and, among the weeds, found a few plants that were barely clinging to life. Knott was able to rescue the berries, which he named after Boysen. He later sold boysenberries from a roadside stand in Buena Park. In order to entice travelers to stop, Knott built cheesy tourist attractions, including a steaming volcano and a full-scale ghost town. Before long, Knott's Berry Farm became more of an amusement park than a berry farm, and so it is today, thanks in no small part to Rudolf Boysen and his boysenberry.

The Heat Is On

At what time of day are you most likely
to witness the Maillard reaction?

☞

Two in the Oven

What's the difference between
baking and roasting?

☞

The Heat Is On

During breakfast. Have you ever wondered why a piece of bread tastes different after you toast it? This is because of the *Maillard reaction*, first noted in 1912 by a French chemist and physician named Louis-Camille Maillard. Simply put, it involves a chemical reaction between sugars and amino acids that occurs when certain foods are browned by heating. The process creates a complex mixture of toasty flavors consisting of hundreds of compounds that change into other flavor compounds as they break down in your mouth. Every toasted food item has its own distinctive set of compounds, some of which are responsible for the difference between, for example, the taste of a toasted bagel and a toasted marshmallow. Other foods that get tastier thanks to the Maillard reaction: malted barley (used in beer and whiskey), roasted coffee, and roasted meat.

Two in the Oven

According to some chefs, roasting starts at a higher temperature, to brown the surface of the food. But other chefs disagree, and the terms "bake" and "roast" are often used interchangeably. Though roasting once meant "cooking on a spit over an open flame," both terms technically mean "to dry cook with convection heat." And while some ovens feature baking and roasting settings, for all intents and purposes, they're the same thing (although most people wouldn't "roast" a cake).

—— DOWN THE HATCH ——

Grub Time

Customer: "Waiter, what is this?
My cheese is writhing with maggots!"

Waiter: "Please lower your voice; the
maggots are supposed to be there."

What kind of cheese are
they talking about?

Prehistoric Hot Plate

How long do anthropologists think humans
have been cooking their food? And what
may have been the first cooked meal?

☞

Grub Time

Casu marzu, or "rotten cheese," which comes from the island of Sardinia off the west coast of Italy. Processing this sheep's milk cheese, also known as *formaggio marcio*, is sped up by the larvae of *Piophila casei*—the cheese fly. Cheese-makers bore holes into the cheese and store it outside; female flies fly inside the holes and lay their eggs (up to 500 of them). Once hatched, the maggots begin to eat their way out, fermenting the cheese into a soupy goo. When it arrives on your table, the writhing maggots tell you that it's fresh and ready to eat. (Dead maggots mean spoiled cheese, so don't eat that.) You can either remove the tiny grubs or just eat them along with the rest of the cheese. But be forewarned: When disturbed, the maggots begin jumping about.

Casu marzu has been outlawed due to sanitation concerns, but can still be found if you know where to look. Cheese lovers swear it's well worth the search.

Prehistoric Hot Plate

Cooking food may go back as far as 1.9 million years. Based on tools and other evidence found at archaeological sites on the African plains, the first known barbecue consisted of root vegetables, beans, seeds, and strips of carrion meat. According to the lead researcher, British anthropologist Richard Wrangham, "Cooking had a widespread effect on all aspects of life—including nutrition, ecology, energy production, and social relationships. In effect, humanity began with cooking."

What a Rush!

On January 16, 1919, the 18th amendment
of the U.S. Constitution was ratified,
beginning Prohibition. Coincidentally,
what alcoholic beverage ingredient
killed 21 people in New England
the day before?

☞

What a Rush!

Molasses, the sugar byproduct used to make rum. And while a little molasses is good, 2.3 million gallons of it rushing toward you isn't.

On that fateful afternoon in 1919, the sticky goo was stored in a massive steel tank on Commercial Street at the Purity Distilling Company in the North End district of Boston. Six stories high and perched on a hill, the tank was nearly full, having received a shipment from Puerto Rico a few days earlier. It was an unseasonably warm January day, about 40°F, and shortly after noon, factory workers heard what sounded like machine guns firing—a noise that turned out to be the tank's metal rivets popping loose. Before anyone had time to react, a massive steel plate careened off the side of the tank and leveled a nearby building. Then the molasses burst out, sending a 15-foot-high wave speeding down the hill at 35 miles per hour. The brown goo covered factory walls, houses, wagons, automobiles, and freight cars, and even destroyed a railroad bridge. Dozens of horses, dogs, and people got trapped in the flood of molasses. Many didn't make it out alive.

The mess took months to clean up, and although Purity's lawyers tried to blame the disaster on saboteurs, in the end the company was held liable for building a faulty tank and forced to pay out millions in damages. This disaster occurred nearly a century ago, but some Bostonians claim that on a hot day you can still smell molasses rising up from the ground.

Multitasker

What do all these things have in common:
glue, asbestos insulation, plastics, aspirin,
synthetic rubber, industrial alcohol, crayons,
chewing gum, baby powder, carpets, latex
paint, firecrackers, paper plates, toothpaste,
wallboard, shaving cream, and whiskey?

Te Kill Ya

Who first put a dead worm into
a bottle of tequila…and why?

Multitasker

Corn is an ingredient in all of these products. Bonus
question: Of all the corn grown in the U.S., what percentage ends up being eaten by people? Answer:
About 1 percent. That's the type known as sweet
corn. The other kind, field corn, is used to feed livestock and make ethanol…plus a slew of other things.

Te Kill Ya

Ancient Mexican tradition? Hardly. And technically,
it's not even tequila that gets the worm; it's *mezcal*,
another type of liquor that's also made from the agave
plant. The practice of placing worms inside the bottles
began in 1950 when Jacobo Lozano Páez, a savvy businessman from Mexico City, was faced with a problem:
The *gusan rojo* worm, which is not a true worm but
the larva of the *Hypopta agavis* moth, lives inside the
agave plant. During the manufacturing process,
worms occasionally found their way into the bottles.
Although the worm is edible and even considered a
delicacy in Mexico, many American tourists were
grossed out by finding a bug in their booze.

Páez's big idea: Put a worm in *every* bottle of mezcal
and boast that it improves the taste of the liquor.
Macho drinkers were all too eager to prove him right.
And as the worm found its way north across the border, along with it came some juicy urban legends: that
the worm is an aphrodisiac, or that it's hallucinogenic
(some people confused mezcal with mescaline, a psy-
chedelic drug made from an entirely different plant).
Neither is true.

—— DOWN THE HATCH ——

The Hole Truth

Why do doughnuts have holes?

☞

The Hole Truth

There are at least three theories, but one thing's for sure: Doughnuts didn't always have holes. Fried balls of dough have been around for centuries in several cultures. The earliest literary mention of "doughnuts," though, comes from Washington Irving's 1809 work *History of New York*, in which he described "balls of sweetened dough, fried in hog's fat, and called dough nuts."

Who was the first person to put a hole in a doughnut? One legend is that Native American hunters showed off their skills by piercing doughy pastries with arrows. Another story comes from New England in 1847, when a sea captain named Hanson Crockett Gregory claimed that he invented the doughnut hole while steering his ship. He had no place to put the doughnuts his mother had given him, so he impaled them on the spokes of the ship's wheel. It worked so well that he ordered his cook to put holes in all subsequent doughnuts.

Captain Gregory's claim, however, is full of holes. Food historians believe the real reason for doughnut holes has to do with surface area. When chefs dropped their dough balls into boiling oil, the outside cooked first. The bigger the ball, the harder it was to cook the inside before the outside got burned, so the balls had to be quite small. The first modern doughnut-makers created the now-familiar ring shape to give us a larger, more evenly cooked doughnut. And for that, we thank them.

—— Down the Hatch ——

Tipping the Scales

If you're an average American adult,
how many pounds of food
will you eat this year?

The Riddler

This famous personality wears more makeup
than a Vegas showgirl, speaks dozens of
languages, and has the job title of
"Chief Happiness Officer," but
many people are *not* happy
with that job. Who is it?

Tipping the Scales

The average American adult eats close to 1,700 pounds of food per year (about the weight of a compact car), which works out to 4.7 pounds per day. If that sounds like a lot, it is. In the last few decades, U.S. annual food intake has increased by 25%. Health officials cite this phenomenon as the cause of the "Great Obesity Epidemic." Of the average adult's annual intake, meat makes up 195 pounds, 57 pounds more than during the 1950s. Good news: Fruit and veggie consumption also went up. Bad news: So did grain products (flours, breads, cereals); Americans eat 200 pounds of them annually, 45 more than in the 1950s. And most of it is refined flours instead of healthier whole-grain products. Not surprisingly, nearly two-thirds of American adults are classified as overweight, up from less than half in 1980. And more than one-fourth today are classified as obese.

The Riddler

Ronald McDonald. He's so well known in so many countries that he's among the most recognized figures in the world. And while health-advocacy groups criticize the clown for advertising less-than-healthy food to kids, he evens out the score (somewhat) thanks to his 305 Ronald McDonald Houses, which are located in 52 countries. Started in 1974 by McDonald's founder Ray Kroc, the Houses help more than 4.5 million kids each year with everything from dental-hygiene tips to cancer treatment.

$picy $tigma$

Up to 75,000 of what living thing must be harvested in order to make a pound of saffron?

☞

Spreading Lies

Throughout much of the 20th century, the _____ industry pressured lawmakers to ban _____. That attempt failed, so they tried to get a law passed that required the naturally white food to be colored pink. That failed, too. The industry's only success: getting a law passed that the food couldn't be the color _____. Fill in the blanks.

☞

Spicy Stigmas

Crocus flowers are the main ingredient in saffron, the most expensive spice on Earth—up to $5,000 per pound. That pound of saffron requires thousands of crocus *stigmas*, the part of the flower that receives pollen. Botanists have bred saffron crocuses to have extra long stigmas, so long that they've become useless for receiving pollen naturally, rendering them sterile. The only way they can reproduce: Farmers must dig up their bulbs, break them apart, and replant them manually. This painstaking work requires hundreds of hours of labor and a football-field-sized crocus bed to yield one pound of saffron. So what does the world's most expensive spice taste like? We're told it's kind of bland.

Spreading Lies

The industry is *dairy*, the food is *margarine*, and the color is *yellow*. Invented by French chemists in the 1860s at the behest of Napoleon III, who wanted a cheap butter substitute, this hydrogenated-oil copycat has long been the bane of the dairy industry. It's naturally white and was originally called *oleomargarine*; yellow coloring was added to make it look like butter. In the U.S., Canada, and Australia, the dairy industry pushed through laws to make sure consumers wouldn't mistake the substitute for the real thing. To that end, yellow margarine was banned in Minnesota until 1963, and in Wisconsin until 1967. Today, margarine outsells butter by two to one.

Ancient Chinese Secret

A more accurate name for the Chinese
delicacy known as bird's nest soup
could be bird's _____ soup.

☞

Through the Grapevine

Wine is manufactured in every U.S. state.
After California, which state
produces the most?

☞

Sack It to Me!

What cynical writer referred to human beings
as "primarily bags for putting food into"?

Ancient Chinese Secret

Did you think poop? Good guess, but the answer is…
saliva. Bird's nest soup, called *yàn wo* ("swallow's
nest"), has been served as a delicacy in China for 400
years. It's actually made from the nests of cave
swiftlets. It takes the male swiftlet more than a month
to excrete enough saliva to form a small cup-shaped
nest that he attaches to a cave wall. After the nest is
removed, the chef dissolves it in water, creating a
thick, gelatinous material that's both tasty and, some
say, medicinal. It purportedly sharpens the mind,
reduces asthma, boosts the immune system, aids digestion, and raises the libido. As such, the birds' nests are
among the most expensive animal-based food sources
in the world, costing up to $4,000 per pound and fuel-
ing the economy of North Sumatra, Indonesia, where
the nests are most commonly found today.

Through the Grapevine

California is the leader, generating 90 percent of U.S.
wine production. Number 2 is New York (3.7 percent), followed by Washington (3.3 percent). The last
state to become a wine maker: North Dakota in 2002.

Sack It to Me!

In his 1937 essay about British socialism, *The Road to
Wigan Pier*, George Orwell—author of *1984* and
Animal Farm—referred to people as "food bags."

AMERICAN HISTORY

*Time to test your knowledge of all things
Yankee, Doodle, and Dandy!*

The Past Menagerie

If you were alive during the latter half of the
18th century, where might you find some
now-famous pieces of Americana that
contained bits of a horse, a donkey,
a hippopotamus, an elephant,
a cow, and a human—but, despite
rumors to the contrary, no part of a tree?

☞

The Past Menagerie

Inside George Washington's mouth. Although he was a strong military leader, the Founding Father was sickly for most of his life—suffering bouts of smallpox, dysentery, and malaria, among other maladies. One of the many medications with which Washington was treated was *calomel*, now called mercurous chloride. That's most likely what wreaked such dental havoc on his mouth: Washington started losing his teeth at just 22 years old, and had only one tooth left when he was sworn in as the first U.S. President in 1789.

Over the years, as Washington endured toothaches, abscesses, gum disease, and painful extractions (sans anesthesia), dentists fitted him with all sorts of toothy contraptions made from the bone and teeth of many animals—but, contrary to common mythology, no wood. According to dental historian Barbara Glover, Washington's first full set of dentures, purchased for about $60, "had a base of hippopotamus ivory carved to fit the gums. The upper denture had ivory teeth and the lower plate consisted of eight human teeth fastened by gold pivots that screwed into the base. The set was secured in his mouth by spiral springs." And this was one of Washington's more "comfortable" sets—most were much bulkier, causing his teeth to jut out and his cheeks to look puffy. Yet despite the dour expression on his face in his portraits (you wouldn't smile much either if you had all that stuff in your mouth), by all accounts Washington was a jovial man who enjoyed hosting music parties at his home.

Battle-hmm of the Republic

Can you hum the melody to an old
British drinking song called
"To Anacreon in Heaven"?

Battle-hmm of the Republic

Sure you can—just go, "Hmm hm hm hmm hmm
hmmmm / hmm hm hmm hmm hmm hmmm." That's
the start of the national anthem of the United States,
"The Star-Spangled Banner." The now-familiar melody
comes from a British drinking song that 35-year-old
American lawyer (and poet) Francis Scott Key borrowed to accompany his four-stanza poem, "Defence of
Fort McHenry."

Here's the story: Two years into the War of 1812
against England, U.S. President James Madison sent
Key and fellow lawyer John Stuart Skinner on a diplo-
matic mission to negotiate the release of a Maryland
doctor being held prisoner on a British ship. Key and
Skinner sailed into Chesapeake Bay from Baltimore
Harbor and boarded the vessel. Once there, the two
lawyers dined with the British commander and eventually convinced him to release the doctor. Only problem: During dinner, the commander had mentioned
his plan to attack nearby Fort McHenry that night, so
neither Key nor Skinner was allowed to leave (so they
couldn't warn the Americans).

From the ship's deck, Key witnessed the "bombs
bursting in air" all night long and felt certain that Fort
McHenry would fall. But then, "by the dawn's early
light," he was overjoyed to see that "our flag was still
there." So that day, Key began penning a poem to
honor the tattered flag. The song became popular
soon after, but it would take more than a century for it
to become the official U.S. national anthem.

Not Like May Flowers

What did the *Mayflower* smell like when
the Pilgrims boarded it in 1620?

Uncivil Apparel

What article of clothing sparked
the Battle of Gettysburg?

Not Like May Flowers

Exactly what history smelled like remains a mystery, but most historians agree that a lot of it stank of human and animal feces. However, the Pilgrims who boarded the *Mayflower* in 1620 to escape religious oppression in England got a bit of a break: Unlike most cargo ships—which reeked of livestock—the *Mayflower* was carrying barrels of sweet wine. So for the first week or two, the *Mayflower* smelled fruity. (No word on what the Pilgrims' ship smelled like at the *end* of the voyage.)

Uncivil Apparel

Shoes—or more precisely, the lack of shoes. Rumor had it among Confederate soldiers that somewhere in Gettysburg, Pennsylvania, was a warehouse full of new shoes. And Southern troops were in desperate need of warm footwear to prepare for the upcoming northern winter. Confederate Army Major General Henry Heth had heard the rumors and ordered his men to loot the Yankee town. On the way, however, they encountered a brigade of Union soldiers, sparking a battle that drew in nearby battalions from both sides. Over the next three days in July 1863, Gettysburg was the site of the bloodiest battle ever fought on American soil— 50,000 soldiers were killed.

Footnote: There was no truth to the rumor—Gettysburg had no warehouse full of shoes.

Moo-ving Right Along

What was the typical pace of an
Old West cattle drive?

States' Plights

Virginia leads the nation—it has seven.
New York comes in second, with six.
Ohio is third, with five.
What are we talking about?

Moo-ving Right Along

Let's put it this way—you could probably walk across the country faster than cowboys could move their cattle across it (unless there was a stampede, in which case the cows moved very fast, though rarely in the right direction). A good day's travel would get the cowboys and their herd about 15 miles from where they started out that morning. Why so slow? Because cows require an enormous amount of food every day—about 100 pounds of grass, even more if they're expending energy (like stampeding). The cowboy's job was (and still is) to know when to get them dogies moving and when to let them stop and refuel, which was often.

States' Plights

Dead presidents. Buried in Virginia are Washington, Jefferson, Madison, Monroe, Tyler, Taft, and Kennedy (the latter two in Arlington National Cemetery). New York City's most famous presidential resting place is Grant's Tomb. Others buried in the Empire State: Fillmore, Van Buren, Arthur, and both Roosevelts. Ohio's five dead presidents are Harrison, Hayes, Garfield, McKinley, and Harding.

In all, 18 states host the remains of former commanders-in-chief. Only one western state has more than one: California, the final resting place of Presidents Nixon and Reagan.

Good-Buy

Did you get a good deal the last time
you went shopping? Was it as much of a
bargain as Peter Minuit's purchase?
No way. What did he buy?

☞

Good-Buy

Peter Minuit bought Manhattan, and according to legend, he bought it "for a steal." But the Indians made out all right, too (at first, anyway).

A former diamond cutter turned merchant explorer, Minuit was sent to the New World by the Dutch West India Company in 1626 to serve as the Colonial Governor of what was then called New Netherland. His mission: to establish a civil government among the colonists, secure land rights from the Indians, and look for goods other than animal pelts to ship back to Europe. History books tell that Minuit offered a few "beads and trinkets" worth 60 Dutch guilders—about $24—to the Lenape tribe in exchange for ownership of the island. But these were more than mere trinkets: Minuit traded advanced European farming technology including duffel cloth, kettles, axes, hoes, drilling awls, wampum (sacred shell beads), and "diverse other wares." And the value was closer to $72.

In a way, it was Minuit who got hosed: The Lenapes didn't even "own" the island; they shared it with the Mohicans and Mohawks. And all three tribes were fighting over who would control the fur trade with the Dutch. Minuit built a fort and a home on what is now the southern tip of Manhattan, and ordered the Dutch colonists living inland to move there, mostly to stay out of the Indians' war.

Although Minuit could make it there, he couldn't make it anywhere: Twelve years later, he was killed during a hurricane in the Caribbean while searching for a good source of tobacco.

Incoming!

Who bombed Florida on
June 8, 1959…and why?

Incoming!

Arthur Summerfield—President Eisenhower's over-enthusiastic Postmaster General. "Gentlemen, we stand on the threshold of rocket mail," he announced in 1959 to the crowd gathered at the Naval Auxiliary Air Station in Mayport, Florida. "Before man reaches the moon, mail will be delivered within hours from New York to California, to Britain, to India or Australia. How? By guided missiles!"

Then Summerfield informed the crowd that the first missile delivery was already on its way—launched only a few moments earlier from the submarine U.S.S. *Barbero*. The missile's nuclear warhead had been replaced with two mail containers filled with 3,000 letters, each printed with a special "First Official Rocket Mail" insignia. (The "official" designation was an important qualifier, because 23 years earlier, the postmaster of Greenwood Lake, New York, had launched an *unauthorized* rocket full of letters 2,000 feet across a frozen lake to the postmaster of Hewitt, New Jersey.)

After flying more than 100 miles, Summerfield's mail missile crashed reasonably close to its target. The letters scattered everywhere, but nobody was hurt, and Summerfield was quite pleased with the experiment. However, few others—including Eisenhower—were convinced that this was a viable way to deliver mail. In addition to the potential dangers involved, the number of missiles needed to transport America's millions of letters every day would have been staggering. Result: U.S. Rocket Mail was declared dead on delivery.

Back for Seconds

Who is the only man to have served as
President of the United States and as
Chief Justice on the Supreme Court?
Hint: He's more famous in the
Philippines than in the U.S.

☞

General Mayhem

What was especially unusual
about the Battle of Palmito Hill?

☞

Back for Seconds

William Howard Taft. The Yale graduate much preferred law to politics, and his lifelong dream was to serve on the U.S. Supreme Court, which he eventually did in 1921, but only after spending four awkward years as president from 1909 to '13.

In the U.S., Taft is perhaps best known today for being too fat to get out of the White House bathtub, but in the Philippines, he is considered a national hero. While Taft was serving as a federal judge in 1900, President McKinley sent him to the U.S.-controlled island nation just after it gained independence from Spain. The portly politician helped set up a new government in the Philippines: He procured millions of dollars from the U.S. in order to jump-start the Filipino economy and to build roads and schools.

General Mayhem

The war was over. During the U.S. Civil War, generals often went weeks without orders from headquarters, forcing them to act on their own. Case in point: the Battle of Palmito Hill, fought on the banks of the Rio Grande near Brownsville, Texas. On May 11, 1865, breaking a local gentleman's agreement that neither side would advance on the other without prior written warning, a Union commander led a raid on a Confederate camp, making off with some supplies and a few prisoners. A two-day battle ensued, resulting in a few dozen soldiers injured and dead. Unbeknownst to them, Confederate General Robert E. Lee had surrendered on April 9, 1865…more than a month earlier.

AMERICAN HISTORY

Freedom Fighters

What island nation's revolution helped
double the size of the United States?

Mapped Out

You may know that the word "America"
comes from Italian explorer cartographer
Amerigo Vespucci. But it was another
cartographer who first wrote
"America" on a map.
Who was he?

Freedom Fighters

Haiti. At the beginning of the 19th century, Napoleon Bonaparte was building up his empire in Europe and extended his land-grabbing to North America. The French ruler laid claim to New Orleans and the rest of the Louisiana Territory. That gave Napoleon's army control of all shipping into and out of the Mississippi River. In short, he staked a claim on nearly *everything* west of the Mississippi.

Then, in 1803, slaves in Haiti revolted against the French colonists who occupied the island nation. Napoleon was forced to send in reinforcements, but his army met with more resistance than anticipated—along with yellow fever—which led to tens of thousands of French casualties.

Seeing an opportunity, President Thomas Jefferson sent an envoy to France with an offer to buy the port of New Orleans for $10 million. Jefferson got a lot more than he bargained for: The besieged Bonaparte offered to sell 828,800 square miles of French-claimed land for $15 million, or about 3¢ per acre. The envoy took the deal, now known as the Louisiana Purchase, doubling the size of the U.S. with the stroke of a pen.

Mapped Out

Martin Waldseemüller. A few years after Vespucci led two Portuguese voyages to Brazil between 1499 and 1503, Waldseemüller, a German cartographer, published the first full map of the New World. He named the region "America" after Amerigo Vespucci.

—— AMERICAN HISTORY ——

Foreign Dignitaries

How many U.S. presidents
were not born in the U.S.?

Bounty Hunters

Who sent the corpse of a "barking
squirrel" to Thomas Jefferson?

Foreign Dignitaries

There have been seven presidents born outside the United States. Doesn't the Constitution require that the president be a natural-born citizen? Yes, but only if he was born *after* the U.S. gained independence from England. The framers of the Constitution added a now-obsolete exception to that rule: A candidate could qualify if he were a citizen at the time the Constitution was adopted in 1787. Martin Van Buren, who served from 1837 to '41, was the first president actually born an American citizen.

Bounty Hunters

Meriwether Lewis and William Clark. Two centuries ago, not long after the Louisiana Purchase doubled the size of the country, President Jefferson tasked Lewis, a U.S. Army Captain, with leading an expedition to the untamed West. Lewis selected his friend and former commander, Clark, to join him. Thier mission: Survey the landscape, find places to farm, make peace with the Indians, and catalog the West's flora and fauna. Beginning in St. Louis, Missouri, in May 1804, the expedition of 33 people set off. Along the way, Lewis and Clark discovered and, in many cases, obtained samples of 178 previously unknown plants and 122 animals, including grizzly bears, California condors, cutthroat trout, magpies, coyotes, and "barking squirrels"—the burrowing rodents we now call prairie dogs.

Terror by Land

A woman named Alse Young was
the first person to…what?

Terror by Sea

What war featured the first
attempted submarine attack?

Terror by Land

Young was the first person to be executed for witchcraft in the American colonies. It happened on May 26, 1647, at Meeting House Square in Hartford, Connecticut.

Five years earlier, witchcraft had become punishable by death in the colonies. Unlike in England, where witches were burned alive, in the New World the punishment was slightly more humane—they were merely hanged (or in one case, crushed to death by a boulder). The historical record is unclear as to what led to Young's conviction as a witch, but it is known she left behind a husband and a baby girl who, 30 years later, was also labeled as a witch. By the time the death penalty for witchcraft was repealed in 1750, 32 people—most of them women—had been executed, including 20 in Salem, Massachusetts.

Terror by Sea

The American Revolution. A Connecticut man named David Bushnell built a hand-cranked underwater craft, which he called the *Turtle*, and on September 6, 1776, Sergeant Ezra Lee climbed into the world's first submarine and piloted it through New York Harbor. His mission: attach a barrel of gunpowder to the side of a British ship, and then blow it up. Lee made it all the way to the ship but was unable to attach his payload. It floated away and exploded in the open water. Then Lee hightailed it back to shore.

Bushnell built more subs during the war, but none of them were able to sink a British ship.

—— AMERICAN HISTORY ——

Attack of the 151-Foot Woman

Where was the Statue of Liberty originally
going to live, and why didn't she end up there?

☞

Attack of the 151-Foot Woman

Egypt. French sculptor Frédéric Bartholdi's lifelong dream was to create a monument that would rival the Colossus of Rhodes, a 107-foot-tall statue of the Greek god Helios that was destroyed by an earthquake in 226 B.C. Instead of a man, Bartholdi decided to create a robed woman holding a torch over her head—and he wanted her to stand at the northern entrance to the Suez Canal, which he'd visited on a trip to Egypt in 1855 at age 21.

Bartholdi spent the next few years honing his craft and drawing up plans. All he had to do was convince Egypt's government to help pay for the statue, which would also serve as a lighthouse. At first, prospects looked good: Egypt was enjoying a windfall from the revenue generated by ships passing through the canal. Plus, Egyptian cotton was suddenly in demand, since a blockade of the Southern states during the U.S. Civil War had halted America's cotton exports. But after the war ended, U.S. cotton returned to the market and the price of cotton tanked...and with it, Egypt's economy. Bartholdi was forced to look elsewhere for a place to put his statue. He chose the United States, a close ally of France. In 1871 he sailed to the U.S. to raise money and to look for a site. As his ship was traveling through New York Harbor, it sailed past Bedloe Island. The sculptor knew he had found his spot.

Bartholdi spent the next 15 years working on the statue, which he called *La Liberté éclairant le monde* ("Liberty Enlightening the World"). It was completed in 1886, three decades after he got his big idea.

Celebrity Endorsement

Who wrote in a letter to Henry Ford,
"While I still have got breath in my lungs
I will tell you what a dandy car you make"?

No Trivial Matter

What bit of trivia was partly responsible for
"The Star-Spangled Banner" becoming the
official national anthem of the United States?

Celebrity Endorsement

That love letter to Henry Ford was penned by bank robber Clyde Barrow, of Bonnie and Clyde fame. Written in early 1934, here's the letter in full:

> Dear Sir, While I still have got breath in my lungs I will tell you what a dandy car you make. I have drove Fords exclusively when I could get away with one. For sustained speed and freedom from trouble the Ford has got every other car skinned and even if my business hasn't been strickly legal it don't hurt enything to tell you what a fine car you got in the V8.

Bonnie and Clyde's business was indeed far from legal—their gang robbed several banks and killed dozens of people, including nine cops. A few weeks after sending the letter, the lovebirds were gunned down by lawmen on a desolate Louisiana road…while hiding out in their stolen 1934 beige Ford V-8.

No Trivial Matter

Believe it or not, we can thank cartoonist and fellow trivia hound Robert Ripley. In 1929 he published a cartoon with this caption: "Believe it or not, America has no national anthem." Famed composer John Philip Sousa saw the cartoon and was surprised to find that it was true, so he decided to change that. After a brief search of possible songs, Sousa promoted Francis Scott Key's "Star-Spangled Banner" as the official U.S. national anthem. His efforts paid off: Two years later, President Herbert Hoover signed it into law.

WHERE IN THE WORLD?

Ain't no mountain high enough, ain't no valley low enough…to keep us from giving you this geography quiz.

Endless Summer

What country has no schools?

Old Towne

Which U.S. town has had people living there the longest?

Land Swap

How many Rhode Islands could you fit inside Alaska?

Endless Summer

Vatican City. Called *Città del Vaticano* in Italian, it was once a part of Rome, but achieved its sovereign status in 1929, meaning that it's not ruled by any other government. And even though it has "City" in its name, it's technically a country.

Covering only .16 of a square mile (less than two city blocks), Vatican City has a population of about 900 people, of which 60 percent are older than 60. Its official birthrate is zero, which makes sense because the headquarters of the Roman Catholic Church is primarily made up of priests, who are sworn to celibacy. No parents means no schools.

Old Towne

It's not Jamestown, St. Augustine, or any other European settlement. The oldest town is Oraibi, Arizona. Hopi Indians settled there sometime before A.D. 1100, and they're still there today.

Land Swap

If you packed them nice and tight, you could fit 429 Rhode Islands (at 1,545 square miles, the smallest U.S. state) into Alaska (the largest state, at 663,267 square miles).

Footnote: Why is it called "Rhode Island" if it's not an island? Because it reminded early explorers of the Greek island of Rhodes.

High There

The 15th step is 5,280 feet! No, it's the 18th.
Wait a second, it's actually the 13th.
Where is this confusing place?

Drier Than a Martini, Even?

What is the driest continent on Earth?

☞

High There

They don't call Denver the "Mile High City" for nothing. In 1890 architect Elijah E. Myers chose a site on which to build the State Capitol building that honors the Colorado city's distinctive elevation. On the stairs leading to the building's entrance, Myers placed a marker on the 15th step that says "Exactly One Mile Above Sea Level." Pretty close, but Myers was off by a few feet. In 1969 the steps were surveyed again, and the marker was moved to the 18th step. In 2003 even more accurate measurements were taken. Now if you're standing on the 13th step, you can be reasonably certain that you're exactly one mile above sea level.

By the way, Myers's other goal was to pay homage to the U.S. Capitol building, so the Colorado counterpart is nearly identical, only smaller.

Drier than a Martini, Even?

Antarctica. But when you think of Antarctica, what comes to mind? Ice, and ice is made of water, right? So why is a continent covered in water considered the driest? Because it almost never rains or snows there. The ice is ancient, and it's still there because Antarctica is so cold: Inland temperatures almost never rise above freezing. In fact, inland Antarctica gets only about two inches of precipitation per year; its coastal areas, only eight inches. It's the driest *continent* on Earth, but it's not the driest *location*. Where is that? (Go to the next page.)

Much Drier than a Martini

What is considered the driest
location on Earth?

Land Lubber

Where on Earth would you have to go
in order to get as far away from an ocean
as possible? Once you got there, what's
the shortest distance you'd have to
travel to get back to the ocean?

Much Drier than a Martini

Did you guess the Sahara Desert in Africa? Or maybe Death Valley in the U.S? They're not nearly as arid as the Atacama Desert in northern Chile. This 600-mile-long plateau, located near the Pacific Ocean, averages less than .004 inches of precipitation annually, and some years it sees no rainfall at all. The hot desert days lead to some amazingly clear nights; there are rarely any clouds or light pollution from cities. Plus, it's at a high elevation. That makes the Atacama Desert one of the best places on Earth to observe the night sky. As such, some of the world's largest astronomical observatories are located there.

Land Lubber

The Dzoosotoyn Elisen Desert in Xinjiang, China. There's a spot there unofficially known as Nocean ("No ocean"). Officially called the "Eurasian Pole of Inaccessibility," it is the most landlocked place on Earth. How landlocked? It would take you three days to drive to the nearest coastline—the Bay of Bengal on the Indian Ocean, 1,645 miles to the south.

The exact location of Nocean wasn't discovered until 1986, when two British explorers—cousins Nicholas and Richard Crane—pinpointed it. If you want to go there yourself, set these coordinates into your GPS device: 46°16.8′N 86°40.2′E / 46.28°N 86.67°E / 46.28; 86.67…and start driving.

How Ya Dune?

Where is the largest area of
sand dunes in the United States?

Continental Division

What's the only country in which
you can travel from the southern tip
to the northeastern tip and end up
on another continent (one that's
not part of the same land mass)?

How Ya Dune?

The logical answer might be in a desert state, such as New Mexico, or perhaps near the ocean—like the giant dunes on the central Oregon coast. But the answer is…Nebraska. More than a quarter of this land-locked state is made up of grass-stabilized sand dunes that are as much as 330 feet high. They're located in western Nebraska in an area called the Sand Hills that covers roughly 20,000 square miles. According to geologists, the dunes were once part of an ancient inland sea that dried up more than 100,000 years ago.

Continental Division

Egypt. Most of it sits on the African continent, but the northeastern part of the country—the Sinai Peninsula—is located in Asia. Turkey and Russia could be the answer, in that both countries sit partly in Asia and partly in Europe, but those two continents form a single land mass now commonly referred to as Eurasia. Egypt, however, is truly a country of two continents. This mostly Arab, mostly Muslim, nation has about 80 million people—95 percent of whom live along the Nile River. It boasts the largest population in the Middle East and the third-largest in Africa.

Footnote: Another country that many people claim belongs to two continents is Panama. However, it's a common misconception that the Panama Canal separates North and South America—it doesn't. According to most geographers, South America starts at the Colombian border.

Mammoth Lakes

North America has three of the five
largest lakes in the world. What are they?
What and where are the other two?

Mini-Mammoth Lake

What's the largest lake in the U.S. after
the Great Lakes? What's the largest
lake after *that* one?

The *Real* Mammoth Lake

Where is the real Mammoth Lake?

Mammoth Lakes

The five biggest lakes in the world:

1. The Caspian Sea, which borders four countries in Europe and Asia, is 143,000 square miles.

2. Lake Superior, in North America, is 31,820 square miles.

3. Africa's Lake Victoria, at 26,828 square miles, is the largest tropical lake in the world.

4. Lake Huron, in North America, is 23,010 square miles.

5. Lake Michigan, in the U.S., is 22,400 square miles.

Mini-Mammoth Lake

The Great Salt Lake in Utah, at 1,700 square miles, is the largest lake in the U.S. that's not a Great Lake. It's the only body of water left over from an ancient inland sea known as Lake Bonneville, which once covered much of western North America. The next largest U.S. lake is Okeechopee in Florida—it's 730 square miles.

The Real Mammoth Lake

There is none. Mammoth Lakes (notice the plural) is actually a geographic region in California's Eastern Sierra mountains. The town and surrounding area are revered for snow-capped peaks, ancient forests, waterfalls, and some very pretty lakes. How did it get its name? Not because of any woolly mammoth fossils, but because of gold: The area was first settled by the Mammoth Mining Company after prospectors discovered gold there.

—— WHERE IN THE WORLD? ——

United Streets of America

What is the most common street
name in the United States?

Fitting In

Cartographically speaking, what do Vermont,
New Hampshire, Massachusetts, Rhode Island,
Connecticut, New Jersey, Delaware, Maryland,
and Washington, D.C., have in common?

Next-Door Neighbors

What's the longest shared border between
two countries? What's the busiest border
between two countries?

United Streets of America

Did you guess Main Street or First Street? It's neither. Answer: Second Street. Why wouldn't First be first? Because a town wouldn't normally have a First Street unless it also had a Second Street (and a Third and a Fourth, and so on). So why aren't First and Second more or less tied? Turns out that many small towns have a main street (often called Main Street) that they count as their number-one route through town— their first street, so to speak, but not their First Street. They actually start counting at Second Street. Subtract the number of First/Main Streets that have been renamed to honor a prominent citizen, and it's easy to see why Second is really first.

Fitting In

Look in any atlas. On the page that has a map of the entire United States, each of these state names is too long to fit inside its designated area, so each one must be abbreviated, or printed off the map with an indicator line pointing to it.

Next-Door Neighbors

The longest border between two countries is the U.S.- Canada border, at 5,525 miles (including Canada's border with Alaska). The busiest is the U.S.-Mexico border. Although it's much shorter than the U.S.-Canada border (1,969 miles), there are about 350 million crossings between Mexico and the U.S. each year. (The U.S.-Canadian border has fewer than half that amount.)

Bottoms Up

It's a nationwide battle for bragging rights!
In terms of elevation, which U.S. state
is considered the lowest of the low?

Bottoms Up

Three U.S. states vie for the title of the lowest, but the answer remains elusive because each state uses different criteria to measure its low-itude. Should the title go to the state with the lowest point, the lowest highest point, or the lowest average elevation?

• Californians lay claim to the title because they have the lowest point in the nation: Badwater Basin in Death Valley National Park, which lies 282 feet below sea level.

• Delawareans counter that California's multitude of mountains elevate that state to a much higher average elevation. They claim that they deserve the title based on the fact that Delaware has the lowest *average* elevation of all the states—60 feet above sea level.

• Floridians cry foul! Delaware's highest point—the Ebright Azimuth near Wilmington—is 451 feet above sea level, whereas Florida's highest point—Britton Hill in the Panhandle—is only 345 feet above sea level. (It's the state's highest "natural" point; some of its skyscrapers are higher.) For this reason, Florida claims that it's tops in the lowest because it has the lowest top in the lower 48.

One reason for the confusion: the board game Trivial Pursuit. In original edition of the game, one of the questions was, "Which U.S. state has the lowest elevation of 60 feet?" The answer was supposed to be Delaware, but the question was poorly worded. It should have said "lowest *average* elevation."

Split Personality

What's so special about the water
in Yellowstone's Isa Lake?

☞

Small and Smaller

What's the smallest nation in Africa? What's
the smallest African nation *not* in Africa?

☞

Range Finder

Where would you have to go to find the
longest mountain range on Earth?

☞

Split Personality

The water in Isa Lake flows in two directions at the same time. How? The lake sits directly on top of North America's Continental Divide. All the rivers and streams east of this dividing line eventually flow into the Atlantic Ocean, much of them by way of the Gulf of Mexico. Rivers and streams to the west of the Continental Divide eventually flow into the Pacific Ocean. Because of Isa Lake's unique position (no other lake in North America does this), its water drains into two creeks—one that ends up in the Atlantic, the other in the Pacific.

Small and Smaller

Africa's smallest *mainland* nation is Gambia, at 4,363 square miles. However, at 174 square miles, the small-est African nation is the Seychelles, an archipelago of 115 tiny islands in the Indian Ocean near Madagascar.

Range Finder

Underwater. Technically, the longest mountain range on Earth is the Mid-Atlantic Ridge, which lies almost entirely below the surface of the sea. It's 10,000 miles long, stretching from the South Atlantic to Iceland, which contains the only part of the mountain chain above water. The longest above-ground, or primarily "exposed," mountain range is the Andes Mountains in South America, at a comparatively paltry 4,350 miles.

FLORA & FAUNA

*Test your knowledge on the finer points
(and quills and teeth and leaves and roots)
of growing things, both great and small.*

Unhappy Feet

What does a spider do when it
gets stuck in its own web?

Humpty Dumpty

What does it mean if a camel
has a floppy hump?

Unhappy Feet

We're talking about the most familiar type of spider web—the spiral web. And yes, it's true that arachnids occasionally get a leg or two (or five) caught in their own webs. To avoid this predicament, most spiders spin two kinds of material: one nonsticky and one sticky. The nonsticky material radiates out from the center, like spokes. That's what the spider walks on. It's also the stronger of the two, providing support for the entire web. The sticky material that is designed to trap prey goes around and around the center in the familiar spiral shape.

So what does a spider do when it makes a misstep and becomes stuck in that sticky spiral? Most species are able to secrete an oily substance that allows them to slip away. In addition, some spiders also have tiny *tarsal claws* located on their hind legs that they can use to slide along the sticky strands to get themselves unstuck.

Humpty Dumpty

Did you assume it's because the camel is low on water? Good guess, but camels don't store water in their humps—that's a common misconception. A camel's hump becomes floppy when the animal is low on food. When camels are well fed, fat cells build up inside their humps, making them firm. After weeks of roaming through the desert with little to eat, the hungry camel has used up most of its fat stores, resulting in a flabby hump.

Even Older Than Mick Jagger?

What is the oldest (known) living thing in the world?

Transformer

Which bear becomes a tiger?

Even Older Than Mick Jagger?

Many biologists disagree over exactly what qualifies as "oldest," "living," and "thing." Some argue that the oldest organism is an amoeba, in that it multiplies by dividing, so each new amoeba is the same living organism as its parent, grandparent, great-grandparent, and so on, all the way back to the very first amoeba. Other biologists point to clonal colonies of plants and mushrooms that reproduce asexually, in which individuals are connected by a root system that has been there for millennia. (There's a stand of Neptune grass in the Mediterranean believed to be 100,000 years old.)

However, the oldest living thing that started life from sexual reproduction (meaning by combining the genes of two "parents") is a tree. A bristlecone pine that biologists call Methuselah has been standing proudly in what is now California since before Stonehenge was constructed. How old does that make it? About 4,850 years.

Transformer

The banded woolly bear caterpillar, common in North America, is known for its brown and black spiky hairs—it looks like a pipe cleaner. The Isabella tiger moth is also common—it has yellow wings with tiny black spots on them. What do these two bugs have in common? They are one and the same—the "bear" turns into a "tiger."

Ear Today, Gone Tomorrow

Why do elephants
have such big ears?

☞

Crusty Critter

What backyard bug goes by many
names and breathes through
gills instead of lungs?

☞

Ear Today, Gone Tomorrow

If you said "to hear better," you have a smart mouth and Uncle John would like to hire you...but you'd be only partially correct. The primary function of these massive body parts, which can reach five feet in diameter in African elephants, is to cool down the animal. The thin ears contain thousands of tiny blood vessels. On hot days, an elephant fans its ears, but it's not the whoosh of air on the rest of the body that does most of the cooling; it's the air passing over the thin skin of the ears, which cools the blood vessels within by as much as 10°F. As the cooler blood flows into the rest of the animal, it keeps the elephant from overheating.

Crusty Critter

A crustacean known as *Armadillidium*. A crustacean in the backyard? Aren't those crabs, lobsters, or shrimps? There are actually two *genera*, or types, of land-dwelling crustaceans, the most common of which is *Armadillidium*. As its name suggests, it has a hard shell, which it rolls up into a ball for protection. You may know it better as a woodlouse or—depending on where you're from—a potato bug, pill bug, chuggy-pig, armadillo bug, doodlebug, or roly-poly. These small gray bugs are usually found in damp places where there's little danger of drying out. There are about 300 species of *Armadillididiae*, and yes, they do breathe through gills instead of lungs. (What's the other common land-dwelling crustacean? The hermit crab.)

—— Flora & Fauna ——

A Crappy Relationship

What species, native to the mountains of Borneo, commonly dines on insects and tree shrew poo, but occasionally kills frogs, lizards, birds, and rats?

The Riddler

I have wings but do not fly.
The fastest horse, I could run right by.
Despite the legend, I hold my head high.
What am I?

☞

A Crappy Relationship

Nepenthes rajah. It's not an animal—it's the world's largest carnivorous plant, and one of the only ones that traps small mammals, birds, and reptiles. Known as a "pitcher plant," *N. rajah* has a foot-long purple leaf rising up over the top of an urn-shaped bowl that holds about a gallon of water mixed with digestive juices. (It looks like an open mouth.) Although *N. rajah* can trap small vertebrates, its primary prey is insects, which are attracted to its trap by sweet nectar on the underside of the leaf. The larger animals that drown in the bowl are just collateral damage.

Why, then, is this pitcher plant's pitcher so large? Because it's the perfect size for a tree shrew—a rodent-like primate—to stand on the rim and eat nectar from the leaf, with its backside over the top of the bowl. Then the tree shrew defecates into the bowl. It's win-win: The tree shrew gets a tasty meal, and the nitrogen contained in its feces fertilizes the pitcher plant.

The Riddler

An ostrich. The average ostrich can maintain a speed of up to 50 mph, making it the fastest bird on land. (By comparison, the fastest racehorse was clocked at 43 mph.) And the story about the ostrich "hiding" by burying its head in the sand is a myth. However, they have been known to lie flat on the ground to avoid detection by predators…before resorting to their awesome speed. *Meep-meep!* (Oops, wrong bird.)

Go Figure

Dolbear's Law—expressed in the equation
TF = 50 + (N − 40)/4—allows us to use
which animal to tell us what?

Range Rovers

Why are there no wild cows?

Go Figure

Dolbear's Law allows us to use the snowy tree cricket to tell the temperature to within 1°F. Found in much of the U.S., these crickets are known as "nature's thermometers." After noticing that crickets chirp faster when it's warmer, American inventor Amos Dolbear first published the equation in 1897 (after he lost a telephone patent battle against Alexander Graham Bell).

Here's how the formula works: TF is temperature (in Fahrenheit); N is the number of chirps per minute. Count the number of chirps in a minute, subtract 40, divide that number by 4, and add 50, and you've got the temperature. (There's also a shortcut, which will give you an approximation: Just count how many times the cricket chirps in 15 seconds, and add 40.) You can do this with other crickets, but each requires its own formula. For example, for the common field cricket, less accurate but easier to locate, add 38 to the number of chirps per 15 seconds.

Range Rovers

We're not talking about feral cows that wander away from ranches, but actual *wild* cows. They did once exist. The animal, called an *aurochs*, was domesticated 8,000 years ago and continued to roam European grasslands until just a few centuries ago. Although the research is ongoing, scientists believe the aurochs was the precursor to the modern cow, though the wild aurochs was much larger than its domestic counterpart. In 1627 a poacher on a hunting preserve near Warsaw, Poland, killed the last known wild aurochs (and had steak for dinner).

—— FLORA & FAUNA ——

Perennial Mystery

According to ancient Greek legend, the
goddess Aphrodite created it. The Romans
used it as a symbol for secrecy (a Roman
phrase for "confidentiality" is named for it).
Ancient Persians spread its oils around the
world. It was found in King Tut's tomb. Early
Christians called it the "blood of the martyrs."
During the Dark Ages, monks kept it alive
for medicinal use. The English fought
for it, and Josephine adored it.

What is it?

☞

Perennial Mystery

The rose, and it's much older than Aphrodite. Paleobotanists have traced its origins to central Asia about 60 to 70 million years ago; the rose remained in the Northern Hemisphere until humans arrived and spread it to south of the equator.

Since the dawn of civilization, people and roses have had a profound connection—for medicinal and ornamental purposes alike. In fact, one of the symbols of decadence that led to the fall of the Roman Empire: Rose gardens began to outnumber food gardens. Some Roman dining rooms even had rose vines spreading across the ceiling. What was said at dinner was supposed to remain there, which led to the Latin phrase for "secrecy"—*sub rosa*, or "under the rose."

In 15th-century England, the House of York adopted a white rose; the House of Lancaster, a red rose. When Henry VII finally won the War of the Roses—and with it the English throne—he bred the red and the white flowers together to create the Tudor Rose, the official Rose of England.

But it was Napoleon's wife, Josephine, and her "Rose Renaissance" that brought the rose into the modern age. She wanted to grow every kind of rose in the world in her gardens. To that end, Napoleon ordered his captains to bring back roses from their conquests. By the end of her life, Josephine had successfully cultivated 250 varieties of the flower. So beloved were her gardens that they sparked a fad of growing ornamental roses throughout Europe and in the New World—a fad that persists to this day.

— FLORA & FAUNA —

Kermit at the Beach

How many frogs live in the ocean?

Miss Hoggy?

What's the difference between
a pig and a hog?

Kermit at the Beach

No frogs *live* in the ocean—at least not for very long. Frogs are *water-permeable*, which means they can drink water through their skin. So if a frog jumped into saltwater, it would quickly become dehydrated and die. However, there is one frog that can tolerate saltwater for short periods of time: the crab-eating frog of southeast Asia. Because the mangrove swamps it lives in can contain brackish water, the crab-eating frog has adapted by increasing its ability to produce and retain *urea* (a chemical compound found in urine), allowing it to absorb moisture back from its own pee so it doesn't rapidly dehydrate as other frogs would, even when it's briefly exposed to saltwater.

Miss Hoggy?

It's all in the poundage. In the United States, any fully grown swine weighing less than 180 pounds is generally called a pig. Any swine heavier than that is called a hog. (This isn't a global rule: All British swine are simply "pigs.")

The U.S. has other specialized names for swine. Newborns are called *piglets* until they're weaned. After that, the animal is called a *shoat* or a *weaner*. A half-grown pig can be a *gilt* (female), a *boar* (uncastrated male), or a *barrow* (castrated male). Adult females are *sows*, uncastrated males are still called *boars*, and castrated males are *stags*. After death, most farm swine get a new name—either *sausage*, *chops*, *ham*, or *bacon*.

Stomping Grounds

How can you tell if two horses are really
fighting or just elephanting around?
Oops…we got that backwards. Second try:
How can you tell if two elephants are
really fighting or just horsing around?

☞

Grass Stains

Rumen, reticulum, omasum, and abomasum.
What are these?

☞

Stomping Grounds

In a play fight, elephants wrap their trunks around each other's heads. In a real fight for dominance, elephants protect their trunks by curling them under their chins while they shove against each other face-to-face at tusk level. Although this battle may seem quite fierce and full of sound and fury, it rarely injures the fighters and almost never leads to a fatality…for the elephants. Humans should keep their distance, though. As the Kikuyu people of Kenya say, "When the elephants fight, it is the grass that suffers."

Grass Stains

Contrary to popular belief, cows don't really have four stomachs—rather, they have a four-chambered stomach consisting of the *rumen*, *reticulum*, *omasum*, and *abomasum*. You'd need a four-chambered stomach, too, if you tried to digest roughly 100 pounds of grass every day. How do cows do it? They regurgitate and rechew the partly-digested grass—called *cud*—as it goes from section to section. The repeated *mastication* (chewing) breaks down more and more of the plants' cell walls, releasing the vitamins and minerals within. Even so, chewing the cud isn't a complete process…which is evident by the amount of undigested grass that gets stuck to the bottom of your boot when you step in a cow pie.

Don't Be Scared

Rhode Island's are red.
Which state's are blue?
And what do they say:
"Cluck," "Tweet," or "Coo"?

And the Sheeple Shall Lead

How many more sheep than people
are there in New Zealand?

Don't Be Scared

If you recognized Rhode Island Reds in the question, then you know they're chickens. And if you know they're chickens, you know they say "cluck." But unless you're a chicken-ologist, you've probably never heard of the Blue Hens of Delaware. The official state birds were once formidable cockfighters, but are now much more peaceful (because cockfighting has been outlawed).

Footnote: Rhode Island Reds are among the most prolific egg layers in the chicken world, some of them producing upwards of 250 large brown eggs per year.

And the Sheeple Shall Lead

New Zealand has tens of millions of sheep—roughly 10 for every one person. Sheep are so important to the island nation's economy that New Zealanders celebrate National Lamb Day every February 15. But with the proliferation of synthetic fibers, sheeps' original economic function—to provide wool for the British textile industry—is no longer their primary use.

So what do the Kiwis do with all those sheep? Many raise them for food. Sheep parts are also used to make lanolin and tallow for candles. Their intestines can be made into sausage casings, sutures, condoms, and strings for tennis rackets and musical instruments. Our favorite: Sterilized sheep poop contains cellulose, making it useful as an ingredient in paper.

—— FLORA & FAUNA ——

Hive Got a Question

You just bought a pound of honeybees.
How many bees do you have?

I'm Gonna Git
You, Sucka!

Female mosquitoes want
your blood. Why?

Hive Got a Question

It takes 3,000 to 4,000 bees to make a pound, depending on how plump they are when you buy them. Who buys bees by the pound? Beekeepers, of course. This recent small-business craze—called *apiculture*—is buzzing with opportunity.

Beginning beekeepers usually buy two to three pounds of bees for their home apiaries, consisting of several thousand workers and a queen. The queen lays the eggs; the workers gather nectar and pollen and tend to the larval bees—the brood. In a good summer, if all goes well within the walls of the comb, the hive's population can grow to anywhere from 50,000 to 80,000. Beekeepers then harvest and sell the honey and wax, and if they're *really* lucky, after all the other expenses (hive boxes, packaging, marketing, protective suits), they can maybe break even for the year. "There's a lot of money in beekeeping," goes an old saying, "If only you could figure out how to get that money back out!"

I'm Gonna Git You, Sucka!

Both male and female mosquitoes feed on nectar, but in order to lay eggs, the female also requires iron-rich nutrients. The world's best supply happens to be found in the blood of plump, juicy mammals. This relationship has worked out great for the bugs, but lousy for people. Due to the spread of blood-borne diseases, mosquitoes have been responsible for about half of all human deaths since the Stone Age.

— FLORA & FAUNA —

That Ex-stinks!

What animal met its end in a museum?

That Ex-stinks, too!

Where did the dodo live and die?

That Ex-stinks!

The Great Auk, a three-foot-tall flightless bird similar to the penguin, once thrived on the rocky islands of the North Atlantic. Then the Europeans arrived. They hunted the easy prey for food and fish bait, but mostly for its soft down, which became highly prized.

By the late 1700s, it had become obvious that the Great Auk was going extinct, prompting some of history's first environmental protection laws, but it was too late. All across Europe, museum curators said, "We must procure a stuffed Great Auk for our collection before they're all gone!" Result: a Great Auk killing spree. On July 3, 1844, in Eldey, Iceland, a museum collector killed the last known pair of Great Auks.

That Ex-stinks, too!

The dodo, a three-foot-tall flightless bird similar to a large pigeon, once thrived on the island of Mauritius in the Indian Ocean off the east coast of Africa. The birds had been living on the island for thousands of years. So safe was their habitat that—over time—they lost the ability to fly. Then the Europeans arrived. When the Dutch began using Mauritius as a stop-over on their trade routes in the 1600s, their ships brought dogs, cats, rats, and humans. The flightless birds were no match for the Dutch and their beastly companions. By 1681, barely 65 years after it first encountered "civilization," the dodo was completely extinct.

—— Flora & Fauna ——

Ichabug Crane

How long can a headless cockroach live?

Skeletor

This common animal has a distinctive feature that is made up of more than 50 bones and even has nerve endings. What is it?

Ichabug Crane

A headless cockroach can stay alive for up to two weeks before it dies of starvation. How can that be possible? Cockroaches are so small that their circulatory system requires no significant pressure to keep blood flowing, so if their heads are severed, their blood quickly clots, preventing them from bleeding to death. And cockroaches breathe through *spiracles*, tiny holes spread around their bodies that require no direction from their brain. And although their brains are located in their heads, cockroaches have *ganglia* spread throughout their bodies. These collections of nerve cell bodies act a bit like little brains, allowing the headless cockroach to stand up, walk, and react to stimulation. Weirder still, a cockroachless head will stay alive, too: It will wave its antennae around for several hours before it also dies of starvation.

Skeletor

It's the turtle, whose shell is technically part of the reptile's skeleton—the ribs and backbones, to be exact. The shells get their distinctive patterns not from the bones, but from the *scutes* on top of the bones, which are made of *keratin* (the primary substance in hair, nails, and hooves in other animals). Although the turtle's upper shell, called the *carapace*, is hard enough to withstand attacks from most predators, it is very sensitive to the touch. (In fact, one of our writers has a pet turtle named Proudfoot that seems to enjoy a good petting.)

— FLORA & FAUNA —

We Ain't Lion

Which African mammal is
responsible for the most
human deaths?

Pocket Protector

A mother kangaroo stands more than
six feet tall and weighs 200 pounds.
How big is her newborn?

We Ain't Lion

When you think of a hippopotamus, what do you see—a fat, lazy animal floating in a watering hole? Perhaps something in a tutu? Don't be fooled: This 8,000-pound beast is responsible for more than 200 human deaths per year; that's more than lions, tigers, rhinos, and crocodiles combined. These massive herbivores are fiercely territorial—especially nursing mothers—and they will attack any human that they perceive as being too close, whether you're on land or in a boat. With its gigantic mouth gaping wide open, an angry, angry hippo will charge an intruder and, in a few documented cases, simply bite his head clean off.

Pocket Protector

The size of a lima bean. That's how small a kangaroo is the *first* time it's born. The kangaroo is a *marsupial*, and unlike other mammal mothers, which carry their young for the full term, marsupials give *premature birth*. After gestating in the mother's womb for about 36 days, the hairless, blind, larva-like, bean-sized baby emerges and instinctively uses its partially developed forearms to climb into its mother's pouch and clamp onto a teat. It stays in the pouch for six months, occasionally poking its head out. Then the baby, now called a *joey*, climbs out and starts exploring but still spends most of its time in the pouch. By month nine, the joey, now weighing about 20 pounds, leaves the pouch for the last time.

What's Up, Chuck?

Oh, no! One of your extremities is swelling;
you have severe muscle cramps, nausea,
and vomiting. Your heart is racing!
You're suffering from *latrodectism*!
What happened to you?

Admiral Birds

In 1916 the French military placed birds
in cages high up in the Eiffel Tower.
What type of birds were they, and
why were they put there?

What's Up, Chuck?

You were bitten by *Latrodectus*—more commonly known as the black widow spider. The condition that results from her venom (only females bite humans) is called *latrodectism*. So what are your chances of being bitten by a black widow? Not high. Although the spiders inhabit much of the U.S. and have venomous cousins in Australia and Europe, none of them are aggressive; they'll bite only if threatened. They live in dark places, so if you keep rolled-up posters in your garage, you may want to open them carefully; if you keep a pair of shoes on your porch, check inside before sticking your feet in. And if you *are* bitten, go to a doctor as fast as you can: Although only 1 percent of black widow bites are fatal, they are very painful and the symptoms can worsen if left untreated.

Admiral Birds

They were parrots. It was World War I, and the French military was taking advantage of the parrots' amazing sense of hearing. That, along with the fact that they squawk loudly when disturbed by any unusual sound—such as enemy planes—made them perfect "guard birds." Placed in cages high in the Eiffel Tower, the parrots could squawk out a warning of a German air raid up to 20 minutes before human ears could detect it. It wasn't a perfect system, however, because the birds were unable to distinguish between German and Allied aircraft.

Good Boy!

If you threw an orange ball into a field
of green grass underneath a blue sky,
a dog would see these colors as a _____ ball,
_____ grass, and a _____ sky.

☞

Wormicide

How many silkworms must die
to make a pound of silk?

Good Boy!

The dog sees a *yellow* ball being thrown into *yellow* grass underneath a *blue* sky. Dogs' eyes, like all mammals', consist of photoreceptors called *rods* and *cones*. We humans have many more cones than rods, which allow us to discern the difference between mauve and lilac. Dogs, on the other paw, have more rods, which allow them to track movement and see in low light better than we can. So, although Fido can't discern colors as well as a human, he's better at picking out movement, so he has no trouble chasing down the ball. Color-wise, dogs can see some of the red spectrum and all of the blue spectrum, but they can't see greens at all.

Wormicide

It takes 2,000 to 3,000 silkworm cocoons to make a pound of silk…and they all get boiled alive. Domesticated 5,000 years ago, the moths have lost the ability to fly and have become dependent on humans for reproduction. When the silk caterpillar spins a cocoon, it wraps itself up in a single thread of silk, which comes from its salivary glands. That thread, which can measure up to 3,000 feet long, would be broken into many short pieces if the silk moth were allowed to emerge. To prevent this from happening, newly spun cocoons are dropped into boiling water, killing the silkworm inside and making the long silk filament easier to unravel. In some cultures, most notably in Korea, the boiled silkworms are collected and eaten.

— FLORA & FAUNA —

The Numbers Game

There are more species of what kind
of animal than any other?

See Ya Later...

How fast can an alligator run?

The Numbers Game

Coleoptera—the beetle. The 350,000 known species comprise roughly one-fourth of all species on Earth, both animal *and* plant. (For comparison, there are "only" about 10,000 known species of ants, and roughly 600 species of primates.) Beetles exist in every habitat except for the polar regions and the ocean (although the whirligig beetle dives into streams and travels inside its own air bubble). Beetles range in appearance from the little ladybug to the African goliath beetle, which can reach six inches long and weigh more than a Big Mac. All beetles have wings, though not all of them fly. So what's the key to their success? They're very strong, even for insects, and are protected by tough exoskeletons. (Uncle John's favorite: the dung beetle.)

See Ya Later...

If an alligator ran past a school zone, it could get a ticket for speeding—the reptiles have been clocked at 30 miles per hour. Still, you don't have to worry too much about being chased down by one on land; they prefer to hunt from the water, where they use the snatch-and-grab method. Alligators only run fast on land when they need to get to the water.

Another surprising alligator fact: Their jaw muscles are incredibly strong, but only for closing. You could easily hold a gator's jaws closed with only two fingers. Try it at your own risk, though, or "Two Fingers" might just become your new nickname.

PAGE, STAGE & SCREEN

One of humankind's favorite leisure activities is to sit and enjoy
things that other people created. Now you can sit and enjoy
these Q&A's about the creators…and the createes.

Head Start

Whose head did Thomas Edison chop off in
1895? And how did it make history?

Hamming It Up

Miss Piggy made a surprise appearance
on a London soundstage in 1979.
What movie was being filmed?

Head Start

Edison's 1895 short film *The Execution of Mary Stuart* had three cinematic milestones: the first dramatic screenplay, the first actors to appear on film, and the first use of special effects. In the 18-second film, an actress playing Mary, Queen of Scots is placed on the chopping block (reenacting Mary's 1587 execution for plotting to assassinate Queen Elizabeth I). After the executioner raises his ax, there's an obvious edit; the actress is replaced with a mannequin. The ax comes down, and Mary's "head" comes off. Then the executioner picks it up and raises it over his head. The end.

Hamming It Up

The Empire Strikes Back. What's the connection between the sci-fi film and the Muppets? Frank Oz—the voice and puppeteer of both Miss Piggy and Yoda. Mark Hamill, who starred as Luke, was a big fan of the Muppets, so when Oz arrived on set, Hamill begged him to do his Miss Piggy voice, but Oz refused.

Here's what happened a week later during rehearsals. Oz was hidden underneath the set, holding up the Yoda puppet, which was "talking" to Luke. "Follow your feelings, you must," said Yoda. Luke responded, "I *am* following my feelings!" Just then, right next to Yoda, up popped Miss Piggy, who exclaimed, "You want feelings? I'll show you feelings, punk! What is this hole? I've been booked in some dumps before, but never like this. Get me my agent on the phone!"

PAGE, STAGE & SCREEN

Bring Out Your Dead

A man gets poisoned and dies.
A woman drowns. Another man gets stabbed
to death. Two friends are beheaded. Another
woman drinks poison and dies. Yet another
man gets nicked with a poisoned blade and
drinks more poison. And another man gets
cut with a poisoned blade. He dies, too.
The last man, same name as the first, is
also poisoned. What are we talking about?

☞

The Write Brother

Claude Perrault designed the front of the
Louvre. What did his little brother Charles do?

☞

Bring Out Your Dead

That bloodbath takes place in William Shakespeare's *Hamlet*. Written circa 1600, the play's full title is *The Tragedy of Hamlet, Prince of Denmark*. Filling in the pronouns from our question (spoiler alert!), it is King Hamlet who first gets poisoned, Ophelia who drowns, Polonius who gets stabbed to death (by the younger Hamlet), Rosencrantz and Guildenstern who get beheaded, Gertrude who drinks poison from a chalice, Claudius who gets nicked with a poisoned blade and is then forced to drink poison, Laertes who (also) gets cut with a poisoned blade, and the younger Hamlet who gets poisoned by Laertes. Tragic, indeed.

The Write Brother

Charles Perrault invented the fairy tale. After losing his government job and pension at the age of 67, the former French bureaucrat decided to become a writer, and began composing moral tales for children. In 1697 he elaborated on traditional folk tales, concocting such stories as "Puss in Boots," "Sleeping Beauty," "Cinderella," and "Little Red Riding Hood." Perrault's book was the first to credit the tales to "Mother Goose." Later, the Brothers Grimm and then Hans Christian Andersen applied Perrault's works to their respective countries' folk tales, which is where we get "Hansel and Gretel," "Rapunzel," "The Little Mermaid," "Thumbelina," and the fairy tale Uncle John most identifies with, "The Ugly Duckling."

Novel Idea

Among Ash-Heaps and Millionaires; *Under the Red, White, and Blue*; and *The High-Bouncing Lover* were working titles for what important American novel?

What Comes Around...

Who were Tristam, Laomorak, Tor, Palomides, Kay, Bors, and Mordred?

Novel Idea

The Great Gatsby. Up until the early 1920s, F. Scott Fitzgerald wrote (self-admittedly) "trashy" novels and plays. Hoping to pen something more important, Fitzgerald told his editor he was embarking on a "consciously artistic achievement." After two years of writing, rewriting, and starting over (and a *lot* of titles), Fitzgerald found his groove with this opening line:

> In my younger and more vulnerable years my father gave me some advice that I've been turning over in my mind ever since. "Whenever you feel like criticizing any one," he told me, "just remember that all the people in this world haven't had the advantages that you've had."

What followed was 1925's *The Great Gatsby*, a sordid tale of wealth, love, betrayal, and bootlegging, set in New York. The book came in at second place in the Modern Library's "100 Best Novels of the 20th Century" behind James Joyce's *Ulysses*. (Would it have been as well received if it was called *The High-Bouncing Lover*? We'll never know.)

What Comes Around...

Along with Galahad, Gawain, and Lancelot, they were Knights of the Round Table. According to legend, King Arthur made them all sit at a round table in order to stop their incessant bickering and start to see themselves as equals. Also according to legend, it worked.

Water You Doing?

The line "I hear things are just as bad up in
Lake Erie" was removed by what author
from what book for what reason?

A Question About Nothing

Why did Jerry Seinfeld insist on wearing
red pants and a blue shirt in the pilot
episode of his famous TV show?

Water You Doing?

Dr. Seuss' environmentally themed children's book *The Lorax* tells of a creature rendered homeless after a greedy businessman removes all the trees. One of the lines in the 1971 book is, "I hear things are just as bad up in Lake Erie." More than a decade after *The Lorax* was published, two scientists from the Ohio Sea Grant Program wrote to Seuss (real name: Theodor Geisel) to inform him of their success in ridding the Great Lake of pollution. Convinced that things were no longer bad in Lake Erie, Seuss instructed his publisher to remove the line from future printings.

A Question About Nothing

That red-and-blue color combo is one of many references to Jerry Seinfeld's pop-culture hero, Superman. One of the most enduring TV legends is that either an image or a reference to the Man of Steel appeared in all 180 episodes of *Seinfeld*. Is it true? Many die-hard fans insist that it is, although some of the allusions are so subtle that it's a stretch. In the first few years of the show, a small Superman figurine sat on Jerry's bookcase; in later episodes, he appeared on a magnet on Jerry's refrigerator. In addition, Jerry and his friends often discussed other DC Comics characters—Lex Luthor, Jimmy Olsen, Aquaman, and the Bizarro World. And Jerry, in his younger years, enjoyed drawing pictures of naked Lois Lane.

Bombs Away

Who appeared on talk shows
in 1987 urging his fans *not*
to go see his new movie?

Bombs Away

Bill Cosby. He could do no wrong in the 1980s...or so he thought. Then came *Leonard, Part 6*. Basking in the phenomenal success of *The Cosby Show*, the comic starred in this spy spoof as Leonard Parker, a retired CIA agent who is called back into action to battle evil vegetarian Medusa Johnson. Her fiendish plan: to brainwash animals (lobsters, frogs, bunnies) to kill people. Wearing a silver jumpsuit and pink ballerina shoes, Leonard ballet-fights evil bird men, and later uses a magic hot dog to foil Medusa. Then he rides an ostrich to safety. Really. According to *every* movie critic, *Leonard, Part 6* was not only bad—it was one of the worst films in the history of cinema.

And Cosby agreed.

He hated the finished product so much that he bought the TV rights to keep it from being rebroadcast (although it's now available on DVD). He also appeared on several talk shows urging his millions of fans, "Don't waste your money." Cosby blamed the train wreck on the inexperience of young director Paul Weiland (who would go on to direct TV's *Mr. Bean*). But it wasn't *all* Weiland's fault—Cosby himself co-wrote the screenplay and produced the film. He won three Razzie awards for *Leonard, Part 6*: Worst Picture, Worst Actor, and Worst Screenplay. Fortunately, Cosby vowed to quit the feature film business. (Unfortunately, not before he made *Ghost Dad*.)

Deduce This

Miss Marple was probably the most famous detective spinster of the 20th century. What offense inspired mystery writer Agatha Christie to create Miss Marple?

Talking Books

How many more copies could a book expect to sell if it landed a coveted spot in Oprah's Book Club?

Deduce This

In her 1926 Hercule Poirot mystery novel, *The Murder of Roger Ackroyd*, Agatha Christie introduced a clever spinster character named Caroline Shepherd. That same year, the novel was adapted into a play. When it premiered, Christie was aghast to discover that playwright Michael Morton had turned Shepherd's character from a wrinkled old lady into an attractive young woman. Determined to "give a voice to old spinsters," Christie decided to make one the lead character of her next novel.

Since then, Miss Marple has been featured in dozens of books, movies, and television shows. She's been played by some very accomplished actresses, including Gracie Fields, Margaret Rutherford, Joan Hickson, Helen Hayes, and Angela Lansbury, whose character on TV's *Murder, She Wrote* was inspired by Miss Marple—a quick-witted woman who has the uncanny knack of always being in close proximity to a murder.

Talking Books

From 1996 until 2010, Oprah Winfrey's Book Club showcased 65 titles. According to publishing industry insiders, having a book in the club would increase its print run by 500 percent…and all but guarantee it a spot on the *New York Times* Bestseller List. The phenomenon was called the "Oprah Effect," and Uncle John is sad that his *Bathroom Reader* was never chosen.

A Star Is Born

What classic novel begins with this line: "The scent and smoke and sweat of a casino are nauseating at three in the morning"?

Can't Touch This

What famous playwright wrote the screenplay to the 1987 crime drama *The Untouchables*?

To the Rescue!

What do actors Douglas Fairbanks, Tyrone Power, George Hamilton, and Anthony Hopkins have in common?

A Star Is Born

That's the opening line to Ian Fleming's 1954 novel *Casino Royale*, the book that introduced the world to Bond...James Bond.

Can't Touch This

David Mamet (*Glengarry Glen Ross*) adapted Federal Agent Elliot Ness' autobiography, *The Untouchables*, which chronicled his efforts to bring down notorious Chicago gangster Al Capone in the 1920s. Other films you may not know were written by the prolific playwright: *The Verdict*, *Hannibal*, and *Heist*, which he also directed. (Whenever Mamet directs a film, he has a strict rule for his actors: no ad-libbing!)

To the Rescue!

They've all played Zorro. The masked vigilante was created in 1919 by New York pulp writer Johnston McCulley. The following year, Hollywood power couple Douglas Fairbanks and Mary Pickford decided that a Zorro picture would be the perfect project to launch their new movie studio, United Artists (which they owned with Charlie Chaplin and D. W. Griffith).

Footnote: Holy swordplay, Batman! Bob Kane, who created Gotham City's caped crusader in 1939, based Batman on Zorro. The play that young Bruce Wayne's parents saw just before they were murdered: *The Mark of Zorro*.

Cheap *Trek*

It's a little-known fact that *Star Trek* creator
Gene Roddenberry wrote lyrics to the show's
theme song. (First two lines: "Beyond the
rim of the star-light, My love is wand'ring
in star-flight!") What's even less well
known is why he wrote them, and
why they were never used on
the show. Do you know?

☞

Cheap *Trek*

Roddenberry's *Star Trek* lyrics were never meant to be heard on the show, but that's not because the network (NBC) nixed them. Neither did the studio (Paramount). Roddenberry nixed them himself. In fact, he only wrote them as a money grab.

The familiar melody was written by respected film and TV composer Alexander Courage. In his contract, it was stipulated that, as composer, he would receive royalties every time the show aired and the theme song played. If *Star Trek* made it into syndication (reruns), which it ultimately did, Courage stood to make a lot of money. Roddenberry wanted a piece of those profits. So he wrote the hokey lyrics solely to receive a "co-writer" credit. (Two more lines: "I know he'll find in star-clustered reaches / Love, strange love a star woman teaches.") As one of the composers, Roddenberry received half the royalties…leaving Courage with only half the royalties that he had expected to get.

Not surprisingly, Courage was disgusted by the deal. Though it was legal, he said, it was unethical because Roddenberry made no contribution to the reason the music was successful. Roddenberry was remorseless, saying, "I have to make money as well—it's not like I'm going to get it from the broadcasts." (At the time, *Star Trek* was floundering in the ratings.) Courage quit the show, vowing never to write another piece of music for Gene Roddenberry. And he didn't.

Commercial Success

Don Draper, the lead character on
the hit AMC drama *Mad Men*, was
inspired by a real-life 1950s ad man
named Draper Daniels. Daniels's
claim to fame: He convinced men
to use a product that, until then,
was primarily used by women.
What product?

☞

Commercial Success

Marlboro cigarettes. Daniels invented the Marlboro Man, a popular ad campaign that ran for 45 years from 1954 to '99.

Like *Mad Men*'s Don Draper (played by Jon Hamm), the clean-cut Draper Daniels chain-smoked, womanized, and often drank his lunch. While working for the Leo Burnett advertising agency in Chicago in the 1950s, Daniels and his team were hired by Phillip Morris to solve an image problem: Since the 1920s, filtered Marlboro cigarettes had been marketed toward women with the slogan "Mild as May." The common perception was that "real men" didn't smoke filtered cigarettes. But new medical studies in the early '50s linked smoking to lung cancer, prompting cigarette companies to promote filtered cigarettes as "safer." That's exactly what Phillip Morris executives wanted Leo Burnett to do.

Daniels had another idea: Don't even mention the safeness of filters. Instead, he rebranded Marlboros as manly. Inspired by a photo of a cigarette-smoking cowboy from a 1949 issue of *Life* magazine, Daniels created an ad campaign featuring "Marlboro Men," which included cowboys, sea captains, construction workers, and weightlifters. But it was the cowboy that caught on. Within two years, Marlboro's profits increased by 300 percent; it soon became the world's best-selling cigarette brand.

Final twist: Two of the cowboys who modeled for Marlboro Man billboards, Wayne McLaren and David McLean, later died of lung cancer.

GOVERN-MENTAL

From neighborhood volunteers to world leaders, here are some questions about politics and the people.

Congressional Smackdown

What's unusual about the gavel used by the United States Senate since 1954? And who broke the one before that?

☞

Seeing Stars

On June 17, 1986, Canadian MP John Nunziata said in the House of Commons, "We consider this to be an item of national concern, and have pulled out the magnifying glass to have a closer look." What was he talking about?

☞

Congressional Smackdown

It has no handle…and never did. The Senate's hour-glass-shaped, ivory gavel is wielded by the vice president in his role as president of Senate. He uses the gavel to begin and end meetings, as well as to maintain order. The original gavel, first used in 1789 by Vice President John Adams, lasted 165 years until 1954, when Vice President Richard Nixon got angry during a late-night nuclear debate and accidentally smashed it to bits. Later that year, an exact replica was given to the Senate by the vice president of India, who said, "I hope this will inspire the lawmakers to debate with freedom from passion and prejudice." By contrast, the wooden gavel used in the U.S. House of Representatives *does* have a handle…and has been shattered and replaced numerous times.

Seeing Stars

Nunziata's announcement came after a concerned constituent wrote to him and claimed that the Canadian five-dollar bill had a small American flag hidden in its design. Conspiracy theorists called it a subliminal attempt to convince Canucks to be more like Americans. Printed in black and white, the tiny engraving *sort of* resembled the Stars and Stripes, but it turned out that the object on the bill was actually a British maritime flag. Nevertheless, rumors have a life of their own, and as such, accusations of American flags hidden on Canadian currency persist to this day.

Work Force

What profession was legalized in Romania
in 2011, and why did that make many
of its practitioners protest?

☞

Nice Benefits, Though

Who was the lowest-paid U.S. president,
adjusting for inflation?

☞

Work Force

Witchcraft. The cash-strapped Romanian government legalized the profession in order to generate income. Now every Romanian witch must pay a 16 percent self-employment tax. Some of the occultists were so incensed that they protested by throwing poisonous mandrake plants into the Danube River. A witch named Alisia complained to reporters, "First they come to us to put spells on their enemies, now they steal from us!" "Queen Witch" Bratara Buzea claimed that she used a dead dog and some cat feces to put a curse on lawmakers. However, at least one witch, Mihaela Minca, was thrilled with the new policy: "It means that our magic gifts are recognized!"

Nice Benefits, Though

Bill Clinton. The presidential salary has been raised intermittently since George Washington was offered $25,000 in 1789, equal to about $1 million today (he turned it down). In 1969 the presidential salary was raised from $100,000 to $200,000. Adjusted for inflation, that netted Clinton around $230,000 in today's money—by far the lowest amount of any president. (When Nixon made that same amount in 1969, it would have been equal to $930,000 today.)

In 1999 Clinton signed a bill that increased the chief executive's salary to its current rate of $400,000 per year, but the increase didn't go into effect until 2001, as the Constitution doesn't allow for a sitting president to get a raise.

And to the Democracy, for Which It Stands

The United States is a republic. Why?

And to the Democracy, for Which It Stands

Despite what politicians always say about "the will of the people," the United States is not a true democracy, but a *constitutional republic*. What does that mean? In the late 1700s, when the Founding Fathers were setting up the new government, they had to decide what kind they wanted: monarchy, democracy, or republic. The idea of a monarchy was quickly quashed because that was the kind of government from which the new nation had just gained its independence. So it came down to democracy versus republic. The founders wanted to set up a system that prevented tyranny—not just by its leaders, but "tyranny-by-majority," or "mob rule," otherwise known as democracy. So they chose a republic.

What's the difference? In a true democracy, the people elect their leaders, *and* the people vote for the laws. In a republic, the people elect leaders who represent them, and the leaders pass the laws. In a constitutional republic, the leaders make and enforce those laws in accordance with a written set of rules outlined in the Constitution. This system of checks and balances ensures that no single branch of government—executive, congressional, or judicial—has too much power. At the same time, it also ensures that "we the people" don't have too much power, either.

More than two centuries on, the Founding Fathers' experiment is still working (for the most part).

Will You Still Need Me?

Which country has the largest
percentage of its population of
age 64 still in the workforce?

Visionaries

What does a British "vision
clearance executive" do?

Will You Still Need Me?

Mozambique. It leads the world with more than 77 percent of its elderly people still working. Due to corrupt regimes, widespread poverty, and the lack of social safety nets, Africa has nine of the top ten countries in which senior citizens are still "economically active." Mozambique is followed by Malawi, Ghana, the Central African Republic, Tanzania, Gambia, Uganda, Congo, and Madagascar. The Solomon Islands—the only top-ten country not in Africa (it's in the South Pacific)—rounds out the list with 58 percent of its seniors still toiling away.

Visionaries

He washes windows. Between the government not wanting to demean public workers, and private sector employers wanting to make their job openings look more appealing in classified ads, the English workforce has become a lot more…fancy-sounding. Result: A rat catcher is now a "rodent operative," a postal worker is a "dispatch services facilitator," a garbage collector is a "waste removal engineer," a receptionist is the "head of verbal communications," a gardener is a "technical horticultural maintenance officer," a dishwasher is a "crockery cleaning operative," and a school cafeteria lunch lady is an "education centre nourishment production assistant." We assume that would make Uncle John a "lavatory experience enrichment executive."

Pressing Matters

Where does the U.S. rank on the
list of top-20 countries with the
most freedom of the press? And
what's the world's worst nation
in which to be a journalist?

Pressing Matters

The U.S. ranks #20. Each year, the human rights organization Reporters Without Borders releases its "Press Freedom Index," which ranks countries by how easy or difficult it is for reporters to do their job. The data comes from questionnaires sent to media centers around the world, who report on "direct attacks on journalists and other indirect sources of pressure." What kinds of actions can lower a nation's score? The government censoring the news, failing to create a safe environment for journalists, or directly harming them. (The PFI doesn't measure how *accurate* the country's reporting is, just how free the journalists are to report it.)

According to the 2010 Index, the seven top-rated nations are all in Europe—Finland, Iceland, Norway, the Netherlands, Sweden, Switzerland, and Austria. For the second year in a row, the United States was #20, up from 56th place in 2006. Britain came in at #19; Canada came in at #21.

What's the *worst* country in the world to be a journalist? Eritrea, located on the Horn of Africa. The government there has closed down all private press agencies since 2001, and has reportedly executed several journalists. Rounding out the bottom five countries in the world for journalists: Burma, Iran, Turkmenistan, and North Korea. (As you'll discover on the next two pages, North Korea is a great place... if you're a dictator.)

Long Game

How many holes-in-one did
North Korean leader Kim Jong-il
claim that he made on his
first-ever golf outing?

☞

Short Game

Why did Kim Jong-il release an
advertisement for a "wonder drug"
that makes people taller?

☞

Long Game

According to the North Korean Supreme Leader, he made 11 holes-in-one the first time he ever played golf. His final score: 38 under par. The unbelievable game took place in 1994 when Kim played a round at the country's newest golf course in Pyongyang. Every single one of Kim's 17 bodyguards swore that his version of events was accurate. Kim submitted his accomplishment to *Guinness World Records*, but so far, they've failed to officially recognize it.

Short Game

It was a ruse. Kim's real goal was to rid North Korea of short people. In 1989 he released a pamphlet advertising a wonder drug that could make people taller. And then, when short people showed up to claim their free "cure," they were rounded up and, according to press reports, "sent away to different uninhabited islands in an attempt to end their 'substandard' genes from repeating in a new generation." What makes this even odder is that Kim himself is only 5'3" tall—he hides it by wearing platform shoes. A few more weird things about the diminutive dictator:

- According to his official biography, Kim rarely defecates or urinates.
- He once tried to end his country's famine by breeding giant rabbits.
- Kim's staff inspects his rice to ensure that every grain is the exact same size.

Shape-Shifters

Who was Gerry? What's a mander?
When did these two combine?
What do they mean today?

☞

Power Play

In Iran, one person has more power
than the president. Who is
it, and what is his title?

☞

Shape-Shifters

Gerrymander is a term that means "to re-divide a state or county into election districts so as to give one party a majority." The term was coined in 1812 when Massachusetts governor Elbridge Gerry redrew Congressional lines in order to give his Democrat-Republican party an advantage over the Federalists. When a Boston newspaper ran a political cartoon showing that one of Gerry's new districts looked a lot like a salamander, the word *gerrymandering* was born. The bad publicity cost Gerry the election.

Power Play

Islamic cleric Ayatollah Ali Khamenei holds the position of Supreme Leader of Iran. He's had the title since Ayatollah Ruhollah Khomeini's death in 1989. (The word *Ayatollah* means "Sign of God" in Farsi.) The Supreme Leader is not elected; he is appointed for life by an elected body called the Assembly of Experts. In addition to functioning as Iran's chief of state, the Supreme Leader is commander-in-chief of the military and heads up Iran's intelligence-gathering and security forces. By contrast, the president is elected by popular vote for a four-year term, but serves at the will of the Supreme Leader. However, the Supreme Leader doesn't have *absolute* power—the Assembly of Experts is in charge of his succession and can depose him if they deem it necessary.

It's Not the Size...

Where do 714 million people use
one million machines for four
weeks every five years?

...It's How You Use It

What two governmental superlatives
belong to the Pitcairn Islands
in the South Pacific?

It's Not the Size...

India is the world's largest democracy, with 714 million eligible voters and more than one million electronic voting machines. The massive country—population 1.15 billion—has 30 main languages, six prominent religions, and a hierarchical caste system that dates back millennia. It has had free elections only since 1947, when the country gained independence from England. In a nation that big, elections are no small task. There are six national parties and 40 regional parties, with more than 4,600 candidates, requiring 6.5 million workers to oversee the process. As such, the Indian elections last for about a month. Within a few years, the nation is predicted to have more people than every other democracy combined.

...It's How You Use It

It's the world's smallest democracy, and the one where the highest percentage of its citizens—21 percent—are directly involved in government. As of 2010, the Pitcairn Islands (the island where the mutineers of the HMS *Bounty* settled in 1790) has 48 residents, 10 of whom sit on the Island Council. But everyone chips in: The public works department consists of every Pitcairn citizen between the ages of 15 and 65. A visiting ship is cause for a national celebration: Every single one of Pitcairn's residents will turn out for a public dinner to honor the rare guests.

Democracy Inaction

What caused an uproar in an Annandale,
Virginia, neighborhood association in
2011 after they elected Ms. Beatha
Lee to serve as their president?

☞

Democracy Inaction

The residents were upset because they didn't elect who they thought they had elected. The vote took place at the February 2011 meeting of the Hillbrook-Tall Oaks Civic Association. President Mark Crawford's term was about to expire, so he asked if any of his neighbors wanted to run for the position. Anybody? Anybody? Nobody answered. So Crawford nominated Ms. Beatha Lee. "She's interested in neighborhood activities and the outdoors," he explained, adding that she "had experience in Maine overseeing an estate of 26 acres." Crawford asked once more if there were any other nominees—there weren't, so he called for a vote. Fifty members raised their hands, and Ms. Beatha Lee was elected association president. Meeting adjourned.

Two weeks later, a newsletter was sent to the 250 families in the neighborhood introducing their new president. The headline read: "Dog Rules, Humans Apathetic (Pathetic)." Ms. Beatha Lee turned out to be a shaggy Wheaten Terrier belonging to Crawford.

Dogs have run for political office before, but people usually *know* they're voting for a dog. Once Annandale residents realized they'd been had, they were foaming at the mouth. "She had a name!" said one. "It wasn't Spot or Rover. It was a *first and last name*! We're embarrassed!" Crawford was unapologetic; he did it to send a message that people should participate more in their local government. He now serves as vice president to Ms. Beatha Lee, who presides from underneath his desk and "delegates a lot."

IT'S SCIENCE!

*Time for planets and atoms and Internets and
nerdy scientists with really big glasses.*

World View

How do Global Positioning System satellites
rely on Einstein's theory of relativity?

☞

Rocky Road

You're taking a walk in a desert and you
find a rock. You say, "That has to be a
meteorite!" And you're correct.
Where are you?

☞

World View

Albert Einstein had two theories of relativity: His theory of *special relativity* proposed that time moves slower when you're moving very fast, whereas his theory of *general relativity* posed that time moves faster in a weaker gravitational field. Those two theories were put to the test in 1990 when the U.S. Department of Defense launched 24 Global Positioning System satellites into orbit. Each one contained an atomic clock that was synced up to an Earth-based system of identical atomic clocks. If Einstein was correct, the time on the space clocks—which are subject to weaker gravity than Earth-bound clocks, and travel at 8,424 mph—should move faster by 38,700 nanoseconds every 24 Earth hours. This seemingly tiny discrepancy would throw the GPS off by about six additional miles each passing day, rendering it useless. So the space clocks were set to account for this discrepancy. It turned out that Einstein *was* correct, and without his prediction, we'd still have to use those annoying folding maps.

Rocky Road

You're in Antarctica. Because of its miniscule annual precipitation (less than 10 inches), it's classified as a desert. And its ice and snow have been slowly building up for millennia with little evaporation. Result: Antarctica's earthly rocks have long been buried under the ice. So if you're taking a walk on the Antarctic tundra and you stumble upon a rock, either a scientist dropped it there or, more likely, it fell from the sky.

—— It's Science! ——

Long Time

The sun is the closest star to us. Traveling from Earth at one million miles per hour, it would take a little over three and a half days to get there. Traveling at the same speed, how long would it take to get to the *second*-closest star?

Short Time

How long is a jiffy?

☞

Long Time

A *lot* longer than it would take to get to the sun. The second-closest star to Earth is Proxima Centauri. A red dwarf too small to be seen by the naked eye, it's 4.2 light years away. Light travels nearly 5.9 trillion miles per year, so if you were able to reach a velocity of 1 million mph, your journey would take 2,828 Earth years. You'd better bring along something to read. (For suggestions, go to *www.bathroomreader.com.*)

Short Time

What type of work you dabble in determines the duration of your jiffy:

• Quantum physicists define a jiffy as the time it takes for light to travel the radius of an electron.

• Astrophysicists define it as the time it takes light to travel one *fermi* (about the diameter of a proton).

• Computer programmers assign it the duration of one tick of the system timer interrupt (between 1 and 10 milliseconds).

• Electricians define a jiffy as 1/50 or 1/60 of a second.

Much about this word is a mystery, even the origin: It was most likely coined in 18th-century England by thieves who used it as a slang term for "lightning." Most dictionaries define a jiffy as 1) 1/100 of a second, and 2) a moment.

— IT'S SCIENCE! —

Krazy Kat

You're in a pitch-black room. All you
have is a cat and a fluorescent tube.
But you can find your way out.
How?

☞

July Madness

In July 1945, Enrico Fermi set up a $1
betting pool at his job. What were
he and his workmates betting on?

☞

Krazy Kat

Create a light source by rubbing the cat with the fluorescent tube. This would also work with your own hair (unless, like Uncle John, you don't have any), but a cat is furrier and therefore more effective. How does this work? Rubbing the kitty scrapes electrons off its fur. Set loose as electricity, they strike the mercury vapor inside the tube, causing it to emit ultraviolet "black" light, which normally falls outside the visible spectrum. However, the inside of the tube is filled with phosphors that—like the special paints used inside fun houses—glow when excited by ultraviolet light. Now you can find a light switch.

July Madness

Fermi and his co-workers at the Manhattan Project labs were betting on the size of the blast made by the first atomic bomb test, scheduled for July 16, 1945, in a remote part of New Mexico. Fermi bet that the air itself would ignite and destroy New Mexico. Physicist Norman Ramsey bet the opposite—that the bomb would be a dud. The winner was a physicist named Isidor Isaac Rabi, who bet that the blast would equal 18,000 tons of dynamite. He was only 2,000 tons short. (Rabi didn't make his guess based on any scientific principle; he was late to the pool and chose the only square left.)

Stairway to Blimpdom

What's the difference between a dirigible
and a blimp? And which one was the
Hindenburg? And what the heck is a
Zeppelin? And why is it made of Led?

☞

Stairway to Blimpdom

A blimp has a soft fabric shell that holds its elliptical shape because of the pressure of the gases inside. A dirigible has a strong frame that maintains its shape no matter what the gas pressure is inside.

The most famous dirigible was the *Hindenburg*, which went down in flames over a New Jersey airfield on May 6, 1937. It killed 35 people onboard and one on the ground. ("Oh, the humanity.") But it wasn't the gases *inside* the dirigible that caught fire; it was most likely caused by a buildup of static electricity from a recent thunderstorm. When a mooring line hit the ground, it sent up a spark that ignited the *Hindenburg*'s paint. (That's one theory—the jury's still out as to exactly what caused the disaster.)

The *Hindenburg* dirigible was also called a zeppelin, named after Count Ferdinand von Zeppelin, who invented the craft in Germany in 1874. For a time, it seemed as if zeppelins could be the future of air travel (as evidenced by the zeppelin dock that was built on top of New York City's Empire State Building), but the *Hindenburg* disaster in 1937 ended that dream.

In 1968 guitarist Jimmy Page played a tape of his new band's songs to the Who's bass player, John Entwistle (or to drummer Keith Moon, depending on who's telling the story). Entwistle joked, "That'll go over like a lead zeppelin!" And that's how Led Zeppelin got its name.

— IT'S SCIENCE! —

The Squeeze

Air is constantly pushing against you, and your body is constantly pushing back. How much pressure are you and the air around you exerting on each other? And what about a soccer ball? How much is it pushing back?

Air Apparent

Clouds are heavy, but they float. Why?

The Squeeze

If you're at sea level, there are 14.7 pounds per square inch of air pressing against you. You don't feel it because your body is pushing outward at about the same pressure. Then, you may ask, why does a soccer ball that's inflated to "5 psi" not collapse in on itself? Isn't 5 psi a lot less than 14.7 psi? It's because the numbers on a pressure gauge don't indicate *absolute pressure*, but *overpressure*—the amount of pressure above 14.7 psi, for a total of 19.7 psi. If you placed that same inflated soccer ball in a vacuum where there's no air pressure, it would expand outward and explode. The same thing would happen to *you* in a vacuum, only it would be a lot messier.

Air Apparent

Even a small cloud covers more than half a cubic mile and weighs upward of two million pounds. And yet it floats. Why? Because there's more than just water inside the cloud—there's air as well. And even though the air is about 1,000 times heavier than the combined weight of all the water molecules, a cloud appears to float because it forms in warm, humid air that's being pushed upward by air currents, and the tiny droplets of water in the cloud take a ride on top of those currents. When the air cools dramatically, the droplets combine into larger drops, and the pull of gravity trumps the upward-moving air. Then it rains.

— IT'S SCIENCE! —

The Not Heard 'Round the World

In the 20th century, two volcanoes erupted
in the continental U.S.—Mt. St. Helens
in Washington, and…do you know
the other one? Why isn't it
common knowledge?

Things That Go Bump

Why do houses creak more at night
than they do in the daytime?

The Not Heard 'Round the World

In May 1915, California's Mt. Lassen erupted, spewing ash several miles into the atmosphere, some of it landing more than 200 miles away. The eruption caused massive avalanches and hot ash flows that wiped out entire forests and devastated nearby homesteaders.

So why isn't an eruption of such magnitude more commonly known in the United States? Two reasons: 1) It happened in central northern California, which was, and still is, fairly remote; 2) the volcano was overshadowed by current events—World War I had recently broken out in Europe. Americans were more concerned about whether the war would reach their shores than they were about a volcanic eruption in the middle of nowhere.

Mt. Lassen became a National Park in 1916, and it hasn't completely quieted down—you can still see its boiling mud pots, sulfur pools, and roaring *fumaroles* (steam venting out of the ground).

Things That Go Bump

Because nighttime is when ghosts come out to play. Don't believe in ghosts? Here's the scientific answer: Houses creak more at night because the temperature drops, which causes the wood and metal parts to contract and rub against each other. This isn't to say that houses don't creak in the daytime; they do, but not nearly as much. In addition, there's often so much going on during the day that it's harder to notice.

—— It's Science! ——

Luna-tricks, Part I

What would happen to a helium
balloon on the moon?

Luna-tricks, Part II

How come we can only see
one side of the moon?

Luna-tricks, Part III

What amazing fact about the sun
and the moon makes it possible
for eclipses to occur?

Luna-tricks, Part I

The balloon would instantly drop to the surface. Here on Earth, it's not that helium simply rises by itself; air is heavier than helium, so the air "slides" underneath the balloon and pushes it upward. On the moon, the gravity isn't strong enough to hold an atmosphere. No atmosphere means no air, and with no air on the moon, the balloon might as well be a bowling ball.

Technically, a balloon on the moon wouldn't even last long enough to fall to the ground. With no atmosphere to push back against its outer surface, the helium inside would keep expanding and burst the balloon, thus ruining the astronaut's birthday party.

Luna-tricks, Part II

Over billions of years, the Earth's enormous gravitational force has exerted enough "drag" on the moon's rotation (the speed at which it revolves around its axis) so that now the moon only rotates once per orbit around the Earth. Result: The same side of the moon always faces us.

Luna-tricks, Part III

The sun is 400 times larger than the moon...and it's also 400 times farther away. Result: The two bodies appear almost the *exact same size* in our sky. So when one of the bodies crosses directly in front of the other, we get an eclipse. The odds of this occurring are truly astronomical.

—— It's Science! ——

Cash for Clunkers

In 1992 teenager Michelle Knapp bought
her grandmother's 1980 Chevy Malibu
for $100. A few months later, she sold
it for $30,000. What happened?

☞

Litterbugs

What is historically significant about a
piece of garbage that was found on
a Wisconsin road in the 1960s?

☞

Cash for Clunkers

On Friday night, October 9, 1992, Michelle Knapp's red Malibu coupe was hit by a meteorite in Peekskill, New York, destroying the trunk of the car. Because it was such a clear night, thousands of people up and down the East Coast witnessed the shooting star as it broke up into many pieces. But the only fragment that did any damage was the 28-pound space rock that struck the Malibu. And that's what made it famous. Knapp sold the car (at 300 times what she paid for it) to a specialty company called R.A. Langheinrich Meteorites, which still exhibits both the Malibu and the "Peekskill Meteor" all over the world.

Litterbugs

Early Wednesday morning on September 5, 1962, a 20-pound chunk of the Russian satellite *Sputnik IV* fell out of orbit and landed at the intersection of Park and N. 8th Street in Mantiwoc, Wisconsin. It was the first man-made object to go into space and then fall back to Earth. No one saw it as it hit just after dawn, but an hour or so later, two cops found the chunk of metal embedded in the road. They assumed it fell off a truck, so they just kicked it into the gutter. But by that afternoon, the news was buzzing with reports of a bright object having fallen from the sky, so the cops retrieved it and sent it to a lab for identification. It turned out to be a piece of history. Today, there's a plaque marking the spot where the Russians dropped their garbage.

—— IT'S SCIENCE! ——

Doomsday!

What would happen to Earth if it were to move three million miles closer to the sun? What would happen if it were to move three million miles farther away from the sun?

☞

Full of Sound and Fury

What was the first man-made object to create a sonic boom?

☞

Doomsday!

Doomsday? Not quite. The only effect would be that we'd put on coats in the winter and shorts in the summer, which we do anyway. That's because our planet *already* moves three million miles closer to and farther away from the sun every year due to its elliptical orbit. That, along with the slight tilt of Earth's axis, is what gives us four seasons. During the Northern Hemisphere's summer, Earth reaches its orbit's *apogee* (the farthest outward point), which is 94.5 million miles from the sun. In winter, Earth reaches its *perigee*, three million miles closer. So far, we've managed to survive unscathed. Now, if some celestial event were to make our planet move *more* than three million miles closer to or farther away from the sun…

Full of Sound and Fury

You might be thinking Chuck Yeager's 1947 supersonic jet flight, but the answer is the bullwhip, which has been used for controlling livestock (and slaves) at least since ancient Egypt. The whip's distinctive "crack" is actually a sonic boom. Here's how it works: A fast-moving object creates pressure waves (like a ship does in water) that travel at the speed of sound, which is 768 mph. When the object—be it a plane or the tip of a whip—exceeds the speed of sound, the pressure waves are all "pushed together," resulting in a sonic boom. Scientists using high-speed cameras have clocked a whip's crack at about 25 percent faster than the speed of sound.

— IT'S SCIENCE! —

Lo Expectations

What's the historical significance of
the following message: "Lo"?

☞

Mirror, Mirror, on the Wall

Why do some objects reflect light?

☞

Lo Expectations

"Lo" was the first message ever sent from a computer in one place to a computer in another place—an important step toward what would later become the Internet. The milestone occurred on October 29, 1969, during the inaugural test of a new computer network. Charley Kline, a student at UCLA, was trying to connect to a computer at the Stanford Research Institute, 300 miles away. He was typing "Login"—but the system crashed after the first two letters.

The project had begun seven years earlier, born out of a 1962 memo written by computer scientist J.C.R. Licklider, in which he visualized an "Intergalactic Computer Network." U.S. Department of Defense chiefs saw the memo and hired Licklider to head up their ARPANET (Advanced Research Projects Agency Network). Lo and behold, Licklider was right.

Mirror, Mirror, on the Wall

It's all about the electrons. Most objects reflect at least some of the light that falls upon them. Highly reflective surfaces, such as mirrors and calm water, have more *free electrons*—meaning that those subatomic particles can easily pass from atom to atom. In other words, they vibrate. Instead of passing the light waves into the atoms (where they're absorbed), free electrons send the light waves back out at the same frequency on the light spectrum in which they came; the light goes in, and the same light goes out. There are two kinds of light reflection: *specular*, which results in a mirror image, and *diffuse*, which reflects only the light energy and not the image.

— IT'S SCIENCE! —

From Here to Eternity

According to futurist Ray Kurzweil,
what advancement could make
humans immortal by 2040?

Fasten Your Seatbelt

Sitting quietly in your seat (or throne,
or wherever you may be right now),
how fast are you traveling?

From Here to Eternity

Nanotechnology. American author and inventor
Kurzweil predicts that microscopic nanobots (tiny
robots) will be zipping through our bloodstreams in
the not-too-distant future, repairing damaged cells
and organs. Disease and aging will become a thing of
the past. Not only that, says Kurzweil, nanotechnology will be able to "back up" our memories to comput-
ers. Every day, Kurzweil takes hundreds of supplements
and drinks 10 glasses each of alkaline water and green
tea—that's so he can stay alive until 2040, when he'll
be 92 years old. If he's right, that will be just the
beginning of his long life on Earth.

Fasten Your Seatbelt

You're moving at about 1,000 mph. That's how fast
the surface of the planet is rotating. But that's just the
beginning: While it spins, Earth is orbiting the sun at
67,000 mph. Meanwhile, the sun and the solar system
are whirling around the center of our galaxy at about
490,000 mph. And our galaxy—along with others
in the Local Group—is moving at 1.4 million mph
toward a region of space that astronomers refer to as
the Great Attractor. Add all those speeds together,
and it's faster than most people can fathom. What
does all this mean on a cosmic scale? In your lifetime,
you'll travel almost the exact same speed and distance
as the average tree.

WORDS AND STUFF

Big words, little words, obscure words, and naughty words.

Fear Factor

What are you afraid of if you have
hippopotomonstrosesquippedaliophobia?

Choose Wisely

A dilemma is a situation in which you must
choose between two equally undesirable options.
What's it called if you have more than two?

Comings and Goings

Study this word carefully: *aibohphobia*.
What is it a fear of?

Fear Factor

Is *hippopotomonstrosesquippedaliophobia* the fear of monstrous hippopotamuses? Not quite. This 36-letter, 15-syllable behemoth denotes the fear of long words. Originally, it was *sesquipedalophobia*. But some clever linguists decided sesquipedalophobia just wasn't long enough to convey the very real fear that some people suffer when confronted with brobdingnagian nomenclature (big words). We don't know who coined this word, but whoever they were, they didn't make any friends with the folks who write the dictionary. According to Philip Durkin, principal etymologist for the *Oxford English Dictionary*, "The *hippopotomonstro* part is clearly someone adding 'hippopotamus' and 'monstrous.' It doesn't really follow linguistic rules. It's sort of a joke. The label actually mocks the sufferer."

Choose Wisely

It's a *polylemma*—like when you're "stranded" on the toilet and you have to choose between your hand, your shirt, and a towel. (Don't you even dare touch that *Bathroom Reader*!)

Comings and Goings

Yo, banana boy—look at it again: *Aibohphobia* is a fear of palindromes (and the word is a palindrome itself). This slang term hasn't yet been accepted by etymologists…or psychologists.

Splitsville

When Captain Kirk said his mission was
"to boldly go where no man has gone before,"
he violated a commonly held rule of
grammar. What rule did he break, and
why is it considered incorrect?
(And is it really incorrect?)

On the Rocks

Etymologically speaking, what do
avocados and orchids have in common?

Splitsville

Captain Kirk split an infinitive—a two-word verb form, most often with the word "to" placed in front of a verb, such as "to go." If you place an adverb in the middle, you've split the infinitive, as Kirk did when he said "to boldly go." Many English teachers, and even a few grammar books, preach that it's wrong to blithely split infinitives. This grammatical conundrum dates back to the mid-1800s when some Latin lovers (the language, not the people) argued that because the Ancient Romans didn't split *their* infinitives, then neither should proper English speakers.

It's okay. Split them all you want. But be warned: Some learned types still loathe it. So if you're carefully writing a cover letter, or you don't want to unnecessarily anger your literature professor, it may be best to move that intrusive adverb elsewhere.

On the Rocks

Both words were named after testicles. The ancient Greek term for that part of a man's anatomy was *orkhis*. Greek gardeners noticed that the roots of a flowering plant they were cultivating looked like a man's *orkhis*, so they named the plant the orchid.

The name of the round fruit, *avocado*, comes from *ahuácatl*, a word in the *Nahuatl* language of the Aztecs that also meant "testicles." (Other words that were possibly named after that part of the male anatomy: *musk*, *edema*, and *cull*.)

The End

What kind of writers are most
likely to commit suicide?

Are You Sirius?

What common phrase came
from an astronomical goof
by the ancient Egyptians?

The End

A 2003 study poetically titled "The Cost of the Muse: Poets Die Young," by California psychologist James Kaufman, examined the death of prominent writers all over the world. Kaufman discovered that not only do writers in general die at a younger age than those in most other professions, but among them, it is the poet who meets the earliest end. Poets live an average of 66.2 years, compared to nonfiction writers, who live 72.7 years—six and a half years fewer than the average American life span. Sadder still, similar studies have revealed that poets have an alarmingly high suicide rate compared to the general population. And it seems that the most at-risk writers are female poets. Kaufman calls this the "Sylvia Plath Effect," named after the 20th-century, clinically depressed American poet who killed herself in 1963 at the age of 30.

Are You Sirius?

The phrase "dog days of summer" may bring to mind an old hound dog trying to beat the August heat by lying in the shade, but that isn't where the phrase comes from. It does have to do with dogs, though. Ancient Romans noticed that Sirius, the brightest star in the sky, rose with the sun from July to August. They thought that the hot summer weather was caused by the added heat of Sirius, known as "the dog star" because of its location in the constellation Canis Major ("Big Dog"). They were mistaken—Sirius is much too far away to heat the Earth—but the phrase "dog days" stuck.

You're in Good Hands

A cartoonist named Sparky coined a
popular term that has since been co-opted
by insurance companies. What is it?

Street Talk

"Hunky-dory" is an American term meaning
"things are going quite satisfactorily."
Etymologists believe it may have come
from another country. Which one?

☞

Well Versed

What's significant about the
sentence "Jesus wept"?

☞

You're in Good Hands

The term *security blanket* was coined by Charles Schulz ("Sparky" to his friends) in his comic strip *Peanuts*, which ran from 1950 until his death in 2000. Inspired by the blankets that his own kids dragged around the house, Schulz gave one to neurotic Linus Van Pelt, and it served as the character's protector and weapon (against his crabby sister, Lucy). In child psychology, a security blanket is referred to as a *transitional object*, acting as a bridge between the infant's total dependence on the mother, and independence; the blanket gives a sense of security when mom is not available. Since its introduction, the term became a common metaphor for anything that provides a sense of security—for instance, an insurance policy.

Street Talk

Dating back to the mid-19th century, the phrase may have been derived from *Huncho-dori*, the name of a legendary street in Yokohama, Japan, that was once known for its, ahem, *friendliness* to foreign soldiers.

Well Versed

If you ever need to memorize a Bible verse for Sunday school, consider John 11:35. Its full text consists of only two words—"Jesus wept"—making it the shortest verse in the King James Version of the Bible.

Jump on In, Guv'ner!

What unit of measurement is derived
from the hugs of old English sailors?

☞

Jump on In, Pardner!

How much water can a
ten-gallon hat hold?

☞

Jump on In, Guv'ner!

The fathom—a unit of measurement for the depth of water. Like many measurements, such as hands being used to measure horses, and feet to measure distance, a fathom was originally based on the human body. In this case, the measurement is based on the size of a hug, from the Old Norse word *faetm,* meaning "embrace." A fathom was originally the length of a sailor's spread arms as he prepares to give a big bear hug; the distance from fingertip to fingertip is about six feet, and so is a fathom. The verb "to fathom" comes from the same word. Dating back to 1620, it means "to penetrate to the depths of the truth, as in, to fathom someone's motives."

Jump on In, Pardner!

If you attempted to pour ten gallons of water into a ten-gallon hat, it would start overflowing after only three-quarters of a gallon. So why "ten gallon hat"? Word historians haven't been able to determine the exact origin, but they think it may have been a misunderstanding of the Spanish *galón,* a term for military-style metallic braiding. The original "ten galón" hats were tall enough to hold ten decorative ribbons. Another theory: It came from a cowboy's sarcastic comment about his buddy's oversized hat: "Hey, Tex, what's that thing hold—ten gallons?" Whatever the case, Old West screenwriters take note: The word only dates back to about 1925.

Department of Redundancy Department

What do these three things have in common: the olallieberry, a thiamine deficiency, and Garrett Morris?

Praise the Gourd

Zucchetto means "little gourd" in Italian. What does this have to do with Roman Catholic clerics?

Department of Redundancy Department

The olallieberry is a cross between the loganberry and the youngberry created by S. J. Harvey in 1937. In the Chinook language, *ollalie* means "berry," so in essence, "olallieberry" means "berry berry." That should not be confused with *beriberi*, a disease that results from a deficiency of thiamine. The word "beriberi" came from either an Arabic phrase *bhur-bhari* ("sailor's asthma"), or a Sinhalese phrase meaning "I cannot. I cannot." Neither berry nor disease should be confused with the 1977 *Saturday Night Live* catchphrase by Garrett Morris as fictional Mets infielder Chico Escuela, who said, "Baseball has been berry, berry good to me."

Praise the Gourd

Medieval monks spent long, cold winters beneath the high ceilings of massive European cathedrals. (This was before central heating.) Making matters colder was the monks' *tonsure* hairstyle—the hair was shaved from the top of the scalp, leaving just a fringe around the edges. Body heat escapes through a bare head, so the monks needed a small cap to cover the bald spot. Ironically, the answer came from the Jewish *kippah*, or *yarmulke*—a skullcap that the monks jokingly renamed the *zucchetto* because it makes the wearer's head resemble a gourd. It's still worn by European clergy. So the next time you see the pope, say, "What's up, Mr. Pumpkin-head!" (On second thought, don't.)

WORDS AND STUFF

Quiet Down, Please

Which came first, books or libraries—
and by how many years?

The Star Report

Why does *meteorology* refer to
weather and not meteors?

Not Joe Mama

Are you enjoying a cup of joe right now?
Bet you don't know who the original
"Joe" was. Turn the page to find out.

Quiet Down, Please

The library came first. Five thousand years before the first books were mass-produced in the 1200s, ancient Sumerian libraries collected clay tablets that contained a variety of information, from business transactions to theology lessons.

The Star Report

Blame Aristotle. He coined the term *meteorology* in 340 B.C. In Greek, *meteora* basically meant "stuff in the sky" (except for birds). So Aristotle called snow *aqueous meteor*; wind, *aerial meteor*; rainbows, *luminous meteor*; and lightning and shooting stars, *fiery meteor*. Over time, the term *meteor* lost all its other skyward meanings except for "shooting star." However, the term *meteorology* has remained—it means the study of rain, wind, lightning, and snow.

Not Joe Mama

Josephus Daniels (1862–1948) was appointed Secretary of the Navy by President Woodrow Wilson in 1913. Good news: Daniels paved the way for women to join the Navy. Bad news: He abolished the officers' wine rations from ships. From that time on, the strongest drink aboard navy vessels was coffee. Either in his honor (or with scorn), sailors later began referring to a cup of coffee is as a "cup of joe."

Divide and Conquer

The mafia has thugs. So do political parties
and schoolyards. But most of these folks
are saints compared to the original
thugs. Who were they, and what
dastardly deeds did they do?

☞

Divide and Conquer

We get the word *thug* from the Thuggees, a centuries-old criminal society in India. Originally called *Thags*, their name comes from the Sanskrit *sthaga*, meaning "deceiver." Killing and robbing people in British Colonial India up until the 1830s, the Thuggees were about as bad as they came.

Their modus operandi: Several Thuggees would infiltrate a band of travelers (who banded together to avoid getting robbed) and pretend to be a part of the group. After gaining their trust, the Thuggees would wait for the right time to strike, when the band was far from the safety of any settlements. Then, usually around dusk, as the travelers broke into smaller groups, each Thuggee would join one of the groups and then wait for a prearranged signal—usually some kind of animal call. When it came, the Thuggees attacked. Using belts or scarves, they simultaneously strangled the strongest member of each little group, quickly and quietly so that no one could cry out and warn the others. From there, it was a simple task to pillage the rest of the camp.

It's said that the Thuggees murdered by strangulation because spilling blood was against their religion. (It was quieter, too.) The murders were committed in honor of Kali, the Hindu goddess of destruction, who was depicted with a necklace of severed human heads. During the two centuries they practiced their "craft," the Thuggees were responsible for at least 50,000 and maybe as many as two million deaths.

Give Them a Hand

˙suortxedibma fo etisoppo eht s'tahW
What's the opposite of ambidextrous?

Secret Messages

What's the only language in history that
was created solely by and for women?

Give Them a Hand

The opposite of *ambidextrous* is *ambisinistrous*, yet another of history's right-handed jabs at lefties. The Latin term for "right-handed" is *dextera*. It came to mean "skillful" and gave us the word *dexterity*. So in effect, *ambidextrous* means "right-handed on both sides." On the other hand, the Latin *sinistra* ("left-handed") began as the word for the lone pocket on a toga, which was on the left side. (Who knew togas had pockets?) The Romans, and many other early cultures, distrusted lefties because they were different. In time, the word *sinister* came to mean first "clumsy," and later "evil." If a Roman citizen was very clumsy, they were called *ambisinistrous*, meaning they were "left-handed on both sides."

Secret Messages

The Nüshu language of China has been secretly passed down from mother to daughter for thousands of years. A written language only, Nüshu has about 2,000 characters. Until it was discovered by outsiders in the 1980s, Nüshu was the best-kept language secret in history. Women used it mainly to write letters, but also used it on quilts, fans, and other decorative artwork. To most men, it looked like nothing more than pretty symbols. Nüshu has remained isolated to Jiangyong County, in Hunan Province, and is known locally as "Dong language." As the literacy rate in China has increased, the language has nearly died out. But some young women are now trying to preserve it.

Net Prophets

How did a fish become a symbol
for Christianity?

☞

Poetry in Motion

What common childhood poem espousing
the benefits of a certain food first showed
up on bathroom walls in the 1600s?

☞

Sleeve It or Not

What do you call the hole in your shirt
that you put your arm through?

☞

Net Prophets

Early Christians co-opted the symbol of the fish for a few reasons. One, the Greek word *ichthus* ("fish") can be made into a loose acronym for *Iesous Christos, Theou Uios, Soter* ("Jesus Christ, Son of God, Savior"). In addition, the Gospels told of many fish-related Jesus stories (many of the Apostles were fishermen). During the first few centuries A.D., when the Romans persecuted the Christians (and used them as lion food), the intersecting curves of the fish symbol were printed on signs to advertise Christian meetings without the Romans finding out.

Poetry in Motion

> *Beans, beans, they're good for your heart,*
> *The more you eat, the more you fart.*
> *The more you fart, the better you feel,*
> *So eat your beans at every meal!*

That's the modern version of the poem. No one knows who made it up, but versions of this ditty were first scribbled on English privy walls in the 17th century.

Sleeve It or Not

Called an *armsaye* or *armscye*, this obscure word comes from Scotland. It's most likely a corruption of "arm's eye."

Dutch Treats

What embarrassing situation
has led to the recently coined
Dutch word *geboortenaam*?

☞

When Bad Words Go Good

What nice word once meant "ignorant,
stupid, foolish, and malicious"?

☞

Dutch Treats

The Dutch Language Union coined the word in 2008 after receiving complaints about a line on marriage forms that says *meisjesnaam*, or "maiden name." When male gay couples applied for marriage certificates, that word led to an awkward moment when the one partner who would take the other's last name had to enter his maiden name. Maiden name? He's a guy—he has no maiden name. In its ongoing quest to rid the nation of awkward moments, the DLU introduced *geboortenaam*, which translates to "birth name."

When Bad Words Go Good

The word *nice* has undergone an amazing transformation since it first appeared in English in the 1300s. Originally from the Latin *nescius* ("ignorant"), the French turned it into *nice*, meaning "stupid." It entered English with that meaning, but over time it was softened to "foolish," then to "wanton" or "malicious." Over the centuries, *nice* took on even more meanings: "extravagant," "elegant," "strange," "modest," "thin," and "shy." When did *nice* become "nice"? Not until the mid-1800s.

In recent years, the word has taken a step back toward its dark past, becoming a sarcastic interjection—such as, when a wayward boomerang hits you on the head and you say, "Nice throw, Crocodile Dumb-dee!"

GAMES PEOPLE PLAY

Time to get on your mark, tee up, and make that free throw through the goalposts in center field!

Stop and Go

A televised "60-minute" football game lasts about three hours. How much of that time are the players actually playing?

Lords of the Rings

Who created the five Olympic rings? What do they signify? And who made them famous?

Stop and Go

If you used a stopwatch to tally up the actual playing time during a three-hour football broadcast, it would total about 11 minutes. (Actual playing time is measured from the snap or kick of the ball, to the whistle at the end of the play.) So what fills the rest of the time? About 20 minutes are spent watching replays. Another 20 or so minutes are spent watching canned video features, cheerleaders, coaches, crowd shots, halftime, and pre- and post-game chatter. Another hour is spent watching the players stand around and huddle up, which still leaves an hour. That's for all the commercials.

Lords of the Rings

The creator of the rings is Baron Pierre de Coubertin of France. Known as the father of the modern Olympics, Coubertin designed the flag in 1912; he chose five rings to represent the five continents (he counted North and South America as one continent and left off Antarctica). Though the flag has been flown in every Olympics since 1920, it became the well-known symbol it is today at the 1936 Games in Berlin, Germany. That's because German chancellor Adolf Hitler flew the flags everywhere he could put them. Newsreels of the Games played all over the world, introducing millions of people to the five Olympic rings…and to the Nazi swastika. (Hitler is also responsible for reintroducing an ancient Olympic tradition—the ceremonial carrying of the torch.)

— GAMES PEOPLE PLAY —

Swingers

Where can you play a round of golf two
miles above sea level? (And no, "Inside a
jumbo jet" is not an acceptable answer.)
What about 220 feet below sea level?
(And no, "Inside a submarine" is
also not an acceptable answer.)

Instant Gratification

What popular sporting event lasts less
than two minutes yet is watched by
more than 16 million people?

☞

Swingers

La Paz Golf Club in the Bolivian capital is the world's
highest 18-hole golf course. Elevation: 10,800 feet
above sea level. There was once an even higher course
in Peru—the 9-hole Tactu Golf Club in Morococha,
at 14,335 feet—but it was shut down after too many
golfers suffered nosebleeds and blacked out. The
world's lowest course—at 220 feet below sea level—
is called Furnace Creek. If that sounds like a hot
place, it is: Furnace Creek is located in Death Valley,
California, where the temperature seldom drops below
90°F in the summer, even at night. Bring water.

Instant Gratification

The Kentucky Derby, horseracing's most prestigious
event. Every year since 1875, on the first Saturday of
May, more than 100,000 bettors and spectators gather
at Churchill Downs in Louisville, Kentucky, to sip
mint juleps and cheer on some of the world's fastest
thoroughbreds. The first televised Kentucky Derby
took place in 1952. At its peak in the mid-1970s,
more than 25 million people tuned in. Though not
as many viewers have watched the sporting event in
recent years (about 9 million fewer), it's still an
impressive feat to get 16 million sports fans to tune
in to a race that is over in less time than the average
commercial break.

Cha Cha Cha

In what sport does a ball "dance,"
and under what circumstances?

Cha Cha Cha

An oddity in the precision game of professional baseball, it's the knuckleball. Whereas fastballs, sliders, and curveballs are all intended to hit a specific target, no one knows exactly where a knuckler will end up—not the catcher, the umpire, the announcers, and definitely not the batter. Batters *hate* knuckleballs: Not only do they appear to dance all over the place, but they travel about 30 mph slower than most other pitches. That makes a knuckleball look tantalizing—like a beach ball floating toward home plate, daring to be swung at. But when the slugger lets loose, his bat usually ends up a foot away from the ball, making him look foolish.

The knuckleball takes such an odd path to the plate because it doesn't spin. That's because of the way it's gripped, with the fingertips. (It got its name because early knucklers gripped the ball with their knuckles.) With every other pitch, the baseball spins so fast that the seams present a fairly consistent surface for the air to pass over. Not so with the knuckler: The seams act like air foils, creating little swirls, or vortices, which cause pockets of low air pressure to form around the ball. Because air always flows from high pressure to low, as it does, it pushes the ball this way and that all the way to home plate—commonly referred to as "dancing." The most successful knuckleballer of the modern era is Red Sox pitcher Tim Wakefield, who struck out more than 2,000 frustrated batters with this devilish pitch.

Gone, Baby, Gone

What do you call a boomerang
that doesn't come back?

☞

What the Flock?

Were boomerangs ever used
to hunt animals? If so, how?

☞

Gone, Baby, Gone

A stick. Or, in the case of an Australian weapon, a *kylie*. Unlike boomerangs, kylies are not designed to return to the thrower. Like boomerangs, kylies are curved, but the curve is less pronounced. (They look sort of like a Nike swoosh.) These lethal hunting sticks predate boomerangs. Originally made out of wood or bone, the kylie was thrown parallel to the ground; it spun quickly as it traveled toward its target. A skilled hunter could kill his prey from a distance of 50 to 80 yards, but if he missed, it was a long walk to pick it up—a well-thrown kylie could travel the length of nearly two football fields.

Footnote: Australian R&B singer Kylie Minogue was named after the Aboriginal throwing stick.

What the Flock?

Although the kylie was the Aborigines' main hunting weapon, it's the boomerang that has become famous all over the world. That's because for most of its existence, the boomerang was used primarily as a toy or for competition. But it did have one use in hunting, and it's quite ingenious: Aborigines placed large nets not far off the ground and then waited for a flock of birds to fly overhead. When they did, the hunter threw his boomerang high in the air so that it swooped back toward the flock, resembling a bird of prey. The birds would dive to avoid the boomerang… and some would get caught in the nets.

Spoil Sports

What two cities in the 20th century turned
down a chance to host the Olympic
Games, and for what reason?

Spoil Sports

Rome (1908) and Denver (1976).

• Two years before the Rome Games were set to begin, the Italian government backed out. Reason: Mt. Vesuvius had erupted near Naples, and the cost of cleaning up after the disaster was too high. That was the reason officials gave publicly. Behind closed doors, however, the decision to not host had been made before Vesuvius erupted. Real reason: The cash-strapped nation simply couldn't afford it. The volcano gave them the perfect excuse.

• Denver's refusal came not from the government but from Colorado citizens. After a state delegation competed for and won the chance to host the Winter Olympics, it was placed on the ballot in 1972. Nearly 60 percent of voters voted no. Their reasons mostly had to do with cost and environmental concerns, but the arrogance of supporters didn't help either: They accused opponents of the Games as being backward, willfully contrarian, and even unpatriotic. Plus, this was the beginning of the Green Movement, and the Games would have been played over a 166-mile span between Denver and Steamboat Springs. People worried about traffic, overbuilding, and an influx of visitors who might want to move there. Also not helping matters: The state government promised that the cost would be capped at $5 million. Opponents pointed out that the 1960 Winter Olympics in Squaw Valley, California, had been projected to cost $1 million and ended up costing $13.5 million. Coloradans decided to keep their money.

Preempted

Why weren't all of the Chicago Cubs'
116 wins in the '06 season televised?

Most Valuable Slayer

Why did the Chinese government ban a
LeBron James Nike commercial?

Preempted

It's a trick question: None of the games were televised because the Cubs won 116 games in the 1906 season. That was the most wins in a season that the Cubs have ever had. The record still stands as the highest single-season winning percentage (.763) in Major League history. The Cubs lost the World Series that year to the White Sox, but would go on win two consecutive world championships in 1907 and '08... and then never, ever again (yet).

Most Valuable Slayer

In the 2004 computer-animated commercial aimed at Chinese youth, the rookie NBA sensation dribbled the ball over two Chinese dragons. Bad idea: Unlike "evil" European dragons, their Chinese counterparts have been revered in Asia for thousands of years. To this day, it's a social taboo to slay a dragon—either real or imaginary. Result: The Nike commercial caused a national uproar in China, not only because James slew the dragons, but also because he dunked on a kung fu master as well as two holy flying women. The Chinese government banned the ad, claiming it did not "respect the motherland's culture." Or, as a Beijing newspaper columnist put it, "What would Americans think if Chinese people made fun of Mount Rushmore?"

—— Games People Play ——

Baffling

What sport, popular in the early 1800s, commonly used a "baffling spoon"?

☞

Men at Work

What sporty fact do all these men have in common: Samuel L. Jackson, Steve Martin, Aaron Spelling, Johnny Campbell, Franklin D. Roosevelt, Ronald Reagan, and George W. Bush?

☞

Marco...

How much older is polo than water polo?

☞

Baffling

The sport was golf—popular in the early 1800s and still going strong today. A *baffling spoon*, also known as a *baffy*, was a driver used to hit the ball down the fairway (the modern equivalent would be a 4-wood). Today, most clubs are numbered, but back then they had much more fun names, including *jigger*, *mashie-niblick*, *brassie*, and *cleek*.

Men at Work

They were all cheerleaders in college (or in Jackson's case, in high school). Who is Johnny Campbell? He invented cheerleading in 1898 during a University of Minnesota football game when he jumped in front of the crowd and yelled, "Rah, Rah, Rah! Ski-u-mah, Hoo-Rah! Hoo-Rah! Varsity! Varsity! Minnesota!"

...Polo!

About 2,500 years. Polo is one of the oldest team sports. The hockey-like game that's played on horseback is a pastime of the upper crust today, but back in 600 B.C., when it was invented by Mongolian cavalry soldiers, it was a warfare training exercise. The name comes from the word *pulu*, meaning "ball" in the Balti language of Tibet. Water polo began in the mid-19th century in English lakes and rivers as an aquatic form of rugby. Today, it looks more like "water soccer" (except players throw the ball instead of kick it). Water polo is widely considered to be the world's most physically demanding sport.

Not Very Ladylike

Who was the only female athlete
at the 1976 Summer Olympics in
Montreal who didn't have
to take a gender test?

☞

Not Very Ladylike

England's Princess Anne, who competed in the equestrian events. Every other female athlete in the 1976 Summer Games was required to undergo a "sex test."

The controversial subject of gender verification first came up in the modern Olympics after the 1936 Berlin Games when U.S. Olympic Committee president Avery Brundage accused two women of being men in disguise. They were Czech track star Zdenka Koubkova and English shot-putter Mary Edith Louise Weston. (Neither were men, but they both later underwent sex-change operations.)

Accusations of gender fraud dogged the Olympics for the next three decades, and came to a head after a 1967 scandal involving Polish runner Ewa Kłobukowska. Three years after winning a Gold Medal, she was tested…and failed. It wasn't because she was a man, but because of a rare genetic disorder that slightly altered her chromosomes. Although Kłobukowska's condition gave her no competitive advantage, she was banned from the Olympics for life. After that, gender testing became discretionary, meaning that only "suspicious" athletes were tested. Apparently, in '76, Princess Anne was the only female athlete who didn't look suspicious. (No doubt her mom, Queen Elizabeth II, vouched for her.) Gender testing was banned in 1999 because it was deemed "sexist, invasive, and ineffective." However, the allegations haven't gone away, and there are talks of reviving the tests in the future.

Whole Lotta Shakin'

You put the golf ball on the tee. You line up
your club. You begin to swing…and an
earthquake shakes your ball off the
tee. Do you get a do-over?

The Disabled List

How much more likely are you to be injured
playing pro football than pro basketball?

Time to Retire

The Miami Heat basketball team has retired
two numbers: 13 and 23. Why is this unusual?

Whole Lotta Shakin'

No matter what the cause—be it earthquake, tornado, falling tree, or maniacal gopher: If you've begun your swing and the ball falls off the tee, it still counts as a stroke. Tough game, golf.

The Disabled List

NFL players are 12 times more likely to be injured than NBA players. (Basketball is the second-most injury-prone sport.) Knee injuries are common in both sports but more so in basketball: They make up about two-thirds of basketball injuries and about one-third of football injuries.

Time to Retire

No player with either of those numbers ever played for Miami's pro basketball team. The Heat retired #23 to honor NBA legend Michael Jordan, who played for the Chicago Bulls and the Washington Wizards. While that's unusual, it's not unprecedented. (For example, every Major League Baseball club has retired Jackie Robinson's #42.) What is unprecedented: The Heat also retired #13 in honor of Dan Marino, the Miami Dolphins' Hall-of-Fame *football* quarterback. It's the only case of a team retiring the number of a player who played a different sport.

HISTORY OF THE WORLD

Hear ye, hear ye: Ye will now be tested on EVERYTHING that has EVER happened in the ENTIRE world (minus North America…and minus most things that happened anywhere else).

High Society

What building had the longest reign as the tallest structure in the world, and what building overtook it?

☞

Well Documented

Which country has the world's oldest still-active constitution?

☞

High Society

For 3,800 years, Egypt's Great Pyramid of Giza was the world's tallest building, rising 480 feet above the desert floor. Built circa 2560 B.C. as a tomb for the Pharaoh Khufu, the Great Pyramid took thousands of workers 20 years to complete. It's as wide as it is tall, with a footprint of 13 acres—the size of 10 football fields. The building that overtook it: the Lincoln Cathedral, an English church completed in 1311. Until its spire blew off in 1549, it was 524 feet tall.

Well Documented

The country with the oldest constitution that's still in use is San Marino, a tiny European nation located inside northern Italy, high in the Apennine Mountains. Population: 32,000. Area: 24 square miles.

San Marino was founded in A.D. 301 by Croatian mason (and future saint) Marinus. Its constitution is much younger, drafted around 1600, but unlike the constitutions of every other nation, it has remained unchanged. Why? Because the country is so small that there hasn't been the kind of internal strife that often leads to constitutional amendments. Besides, no armies have ever thought to invade San Marino, which also could have led to changes in its constitution; it's too isolated and has no significant bodies of water or even any level land (except for soccer fields). Locals, however, credit the nation's stability to its serene setting. How serene? The country's official name is the Most Serene Republic of San Marino.

Say It Loud

What declaration made
celebrities out of Hiroo Onoda
and Teruo Nakamura in 1974?

Say It Loud

Nearly 30 years after World War II ended, the last two Japanese soldiers finally formally surrendered. Hiroo Onoda and Teruo Nakamura had both been assigned to remote posts—Onoda in the Philippines and Nakamura in Indonesia. After Japan's defeat, they were believed to be dead, but they soldiered on.

Onoda, an intelligence officer and saboteur, led a dwindling band of holdouts in mini-battle campaigns against Filipino farmers, who tried—to no avail—to convince Onoda and his men that the war was over. The farmers fought back until Onoda was the only one left. He lived alone in the woods, and would have died there had it not been for a Japanese college dropout named Norio Suzuki, who told his friends he was going to find "Lieutenant Onoda, a panda, and the Abominable Snowman, in that order." In early 1974, Suzuki did find Onoda and the two became friends, but Onoda *still* refused to surrender…unless he was ordered to do so by his superior officer. So Suzuki returned to Japan and told his tale to the government. Officials tracked down the soldier's ex-commander, who now owned a bookstore, and flew him to the Philippines. He ordered Onoda to surrender.

A few months after Onoda toured Japan as the "last World War II soldier," Teruo Nakamura was spotted by a pilot who noticed a small camp in the middle of the Indonesian wilderness. He took a bit of convincing as well, but surrendered a short time later. Both men were given back pay and a modest pension.

By Any Other Name

Uncle John's original surname was
Poopenheimer, but he changed it out of
embarrassment. (He now regrets that change.)
In 1917 the British Royal Family also changed
their surname. What did they change it
from (not Poopenheimer), and why?

☞

Native Tongue

What were *ientaculum*, *praendium*,
merenda, and *cena*?

☞

By Any Other Name

The British Royal Family's surname was once Saxe-Coburg-Gotha, a name it shared with many European royal houses. During World War I, while England was mired in a fierce conflict with Germany, the Royal Family decided that a less German-sounding surname might ease tensions at home. So in 1917 they changed their name to the more British-sounding House of Windsor, after one of their many royal homes, Windsor Castle.

Native Tongue

Ancient Roman mealtimes. With more time on their hands than most of us have today, well-to-do Romans enjoyed four meals a day. What we'd call breakfast was *ientaculum*, followed by a lunch-like *praendium*. *Merenda* was a light afternoon meal comparable to the British tea time, and then came *cena* (supper).

A family dining by themselves might take an hour for a *cena* of fruits, vegetables, breads, and grain porridge. However, if the family were hosting company, they were expected to provide a multiple-course extravaganza with a rich variety of wines and exotic foods—ostrich, peacock, or boiled dormice (a bird) dipped in honey and poppy seeds. These lavish *cenas* could last up to four hours.

Footnote: Rome was the first city in history to have more than one million citizens. The next city to achieve that feat was London in the 1800s.

The Papal Chase

In the history of the Roman Catholic
Church, only one man served as pope
three separate times. Who was he?

☞

The Papal Chase

Pope Benedict IX (1012–56)—arguably the worst pope ever. How bad was he? According to a later Pope, Victor III, Benedict IX committed "rapes, murders and other unspeakable acts." (Those "other unspeakable acts" were, reportedly, bestiality.) How could such a horrible man ascend to a level of such prominence three times? Corruption.

Benedict was born Theophylactus of Tusculum into a wealthy Roman family, and two of his uncles had previously served as pope. His rich father basically bought Benedict the papacy—through bribes and political pressure—in 1032 when Benedict was a teenager. Unspeakable acts commenced.

Four years later, Benedict was forced out of Rome by outraged clerics, only to return a few months later and forcibly retake his position. In 1044 he was deposed again…until his armed forces regained control. Less than a year later, Benedict had grown tired of the job, so he sold the papacy to one of his uncles. Soon after, he changed his mind and took it back by force. By this point, Holy Roman Emperor Henry III had tired of all the papal shenanigans and ordered his army to remove Benedict once and for all. Henry then promoted John, bishop of Sabinato, to pope (John served as Sylvester III and was later charged with bribing his way into the position). Meanwhile, the excommunicated Benedict slunk home to Tusculum as just Theophylactus again. And then he died.

Afterlife Savings

How did Ancient Egyptians prepare the
brains of the deceased for mummification?

☞

Burning Irony

How did the Great London Fire of 1666
save more human lives than it took?

☞

Afterlife Savings

The Egyptians didn't care about the brain. They believed that the heart was the source of thought and feeling, and that the brain was an insignificant mass of tissue. Before carefully preparing the heart, liver, intestines, and other vital organs for the trip to the next world, Egyptian embalmers inserted a type of whisk into the cranium through the dead person's nostril and then whipped the brain into a gooey liquid for easy extraction—also through the nose.

Burning Irony

In 1666 the Great London Fire started in a bakery on Pudding Lane and burned for several days. By the time it was out, 80 percent of London's structures were gone, leaving tens of thousands of people homeless. Although only a handful of deaths were reported, there were probably many more because most of the dead were peasants, and they weren't counted.

But one thing is known—untold thousands of lives were saved. How? The fire occurred not long after a breakout of the bubonic plague. The plague was spread by fleas that jumped from rats to humans. The rats, in turn, lived in London's homes and other buildings. After the fire, with most of the buildings gone, the vermin had no place to hide…and became easy prey for London's hungry dogs and cats. Result: The plague outbreak ended.

Unholy Matrimony

Two world conquerors, centuries apart.
One from the East and one from the West.
Two weddings. Two disastrous wedding
nights. Who were they?

Urban Sprawl

What ancient city's population grew
so large that its leaders literally
expanded the ground beneath it?

Unholy Matrimony

Attila the Hun and Napoleon Bonaparte. On Napoleon's wedding night in 1796, Josephine insisted on letting her dog—a pug named Fortuné—sleep in the bed with them. When Napoleon climbed in to the bed, Fortuné bit him on the leg, leaving the French conqueror terrified that he'd contracted rabies. Napoleon didn't get rabies, but his one-night relationship with dogs was over. (He was, in fact, a cat person, and later enacted a law that no French dogs could ever be named "Napoleon.")

At least Napoleon *survived* his honeymoon. In A.D. 453, Attila the Hun wed a young woman named Ildico. After the wedding, Attila hosted a feast that lasted long into the night. When Ildico awoke the next morning, she discovered Attila's lifeless body. Although some historians believe that he may have been murdered, most say the death was accidental: Attila likely suffered one of his chronic nosebleeds and was so drunk that he didn't wake up…and drowned in his own blood.

Urban Sprawl

The Aztec city of Tenochtitlan. Built in the early 1300s, the city was home to 60,000 people. That was way too many for its location—an island in what is now Mexico's Lake Texcoco. Solution: The people built large rafts from wood, covered them in mud, and used stakes to secure them to the lakebed. The floating outskirts supported homes and farmland.

The Riddler

The Romans first built it out of wood 2,000 years ago. A Norwegian prince named Olaf tore it down 1,000 years after that. It was rebuilt, then destroyed by a storm, and then rebuilt again, only to be destroyed by a fire. Roughly 500 years ago, a stone version was built that included homes, businesses, and a church. In the 1960s, it was moved thousands of miles away. Then it was rebuilt yet again near its original spot. What is it?

☞

The Riddler

London Bridge—and yes, it has fallen down quite a few times over the years.

The bridge has had a storied history, to say the least. From the 1300s to the 1600s, the heads of England's slain enemies—including, most famously, William Wallace and Thomas More—were displayed on the Stone Gateway on the bridge's southern end. During that time, London Bridge was a bustling little village in its own right: Thousands of people passed over it and under it, lived inside homes that were built on top of it, shopped in its stores, and worshipped in its churches. (But there were no food stores, because there were no cellars to keep food cool.) It became so crowded that a separate bridge was erected nearby for pedestrians who needed to get over the river quickly.

After nearly sinking into the Thames because the foundation couldn't support all of the weight, London Bridge was rebuilt yet again in 1831. The first ship to pass underneath it was the HMS *Beagle*, later made famous by the explorations of Charles Darwin. The bridge was replaced again in the 1920s, and yet again in 1962 after an American named Robert McCulloch purchased the old one for $2.5 million and moved it piece by piece to Lake Havasu City in Arizona (*Guinness World Records* lists it as the "world's largest antique"). A new London Bridge was built in 1973 out of steel and concrete. Although it lacks the splendor of its glory days, thousands of people still cross London Bridge every day—just as they have for centuries.

Joe Ming?

Who was China's Ming
Dynasty named after?

The Wrath of Kon

Archaeologists trace the beginning of
the Inca Empire back to A.D. 1150 in
the Cuzco valley, now Peru. According
to an Inca creation myth, why are
the jungles full of monkeys?

Joe Ming?

That's a trick question, because *Ming* was not a man but an adjective: It's the Chinese word for "brilliant."

In 1368 a Buddhist monk named Zhu Yuanzhang led a peasant rebellion that toppled the Mongol-ruled Yuan Dynasty, which was oppressing and overtaxing the ethnic Han people. For the next three centuries, Yuanzhang's "brilliant" dynasty lived up to the name: Slavery was abolished, and peace, technology, wealth, and artistry flourished.

The Wrath of Kon

There are two Inca creation myths, both revolving around a god named Kon Tiki. In one myth, he was benevolent and began civilization. End of story. In the other, he took the form of a boneless man and created the sun, called Inti, as well as the first people and everything they needed to thrive. But over time, the people forgot about Kon Tiki's gifts and rebelled against him. So Kon Tiki stopped the rain from falling, sending famine throughout the "Four Corners of the Earth," as the region was called by its citizens. While the people lay dying, a new god emerged called Pachachamac. He battled Kon Tiki and drove him away…and turned the dying people into monkeys. Then Pachachamac created the Inca people, who (along with the monkeys in the forests) flourished for centuries. Then the Spanish arrived in South America and virtually wiped out the Incan culture.

Mother of Invention

What did a Japanese madame named
Izumo no Okuni invent in the 1600s?

☞

Satan Claus

Who is Santa Claus's evil counterpart?

☞

Mother of Invention

Kabuki theater, a precursor to modern musical theater. Okuni was a Shinto priestess (and rumored brothel owner) who trained her ladies to perform the first Kabuki plays in the dry river beds of Kyoto. The women played both male and female roles. The plays remained popular for three decades until women were banned from performing. Kabuki theater went on, but with men performing all the roles, which was seen as less scandalous. In the 20th century, women once again returned to the Kabuki stage.

Satan Claus

In Alpine European traditions dating back to pre-Christian times, there have been tales of "wild men" roaming the forests. One of these Pagan anti-heroes was turned into Santa's satanic counterpart—the anti-Claus, as it were. His name is Krampus. The word comes from the German tern *krampen*, meaning "claw" (but it has nothing to do with the *Claus* in "Santa Claus"). Demonic in nature and appearance, Krampus has a snarling goatlike face, sharp teeth, and curved horns. He accompanies Santa on his Christmas journey, but instead of bringing gifts to the good kids, Krampus carries a collection of bad things for the naughty ones—switches, nightmares, and beatings.

Well, he used to. In recent years, Krampus has been deemed too scary for kids, so grown-up Austrians have adopted him as their mascot for a boozy three-day weekend at the beginning of December known as *Krampustag.*

Really?

Whose head did Elizabeth
Throckmorton carry around in
a leather satchel for 29 years?

☞

Really?

The embalmed head of her husband, Sir Walter Raleigh.

Before he lost his head, Raleigh, born in 1552, was a well-to-do English admiral, politician, explorer, and aristocrat. Most famously, he brought tobacco back from an expedition to the New World and popularized it among London's elite. At the age of 28, Raleigh became a favorite courtier of Queen Elizabeth I and later named the Colony of Virginia after her (Elizabeth was known as "The Virgin Queen"). But Raleigh's true love was the queen's handmaiden, Elizabeth Throckmorton. The two secretly married in 1592. When the queen found out, she was devastated and briefly imprisoned the couple. After their release, Raleigh tried to win back Her Majesty's favor by leading an expedition to find a legendary gold-rich land known as El Dorado in Venezuela. He failed.

The queen's successor, King James I, disliked Raleigh and in 1600 imprisoned him for an alleged plot to overthrow the monarchy. After serving 12 years of a life sentence, Raleigh was given another chance to redeem himself. He set sail again to find El Dorado…and failed again. Even worse, he attacked some Spanish soldiers against James's orders. Relations with the Spanish were strained, so in 1618, Raleigh, now 66 years old, was made an example of and beheaded. Throckmorton was inconsolable: She kept his embalmed head in her satchel for three decades until she died in 1647. Then the head was reunited with the rest of his corpse. You can visit both in the church of St. Margaret's, Westminster.

Tick Tock

If Earth's history were squeezed into
one year, at what time on what
day would humans appear?

☞

Tick Tock

If Earth's entire history were compressed into one 365-day year, modern humans wouldn't show up until about 15 minutes to midnight on December 31.

This calculation is based on the prevailing theory that Earth is 4.6 billion years old. So, by this model, our planet was "born" on January 1 when it solidified into a ball. After a few "months" (a billion years or so) of wind and rain wearing down mountains and creating oceans, bacteria came along in late March. In June, most of North America was still underwater. In July, the first plant life appeared. In August, the first fish. In September, the first insects. Starting in October, the dinosaurs ruled for about a month. Then, right around the time a huge asteroid hit Earth just after Thanksgiving, the dinosaurs disappeared. On Christmas, the Colorado River began its long, slow process of carving the Grand Canyon. The first true mammals didn't scurry about until sometime on December 28.

Finally, at noon on New Year's Eve, hominids started standing up on their own two feet. At 11:00 p.m., the Neanderthals showed up. Modern humans didn't join the party until 11:45 p.m., and they didn't start building cities until about 11:55. At about 20 seconds to midnight, Columbus sailed the ocean blue. The next five centuries—though a blip on the geologic timescale—have seen a lot of things change on planet Earth. Let's see what happens next year!

287

UNCLE JOHN'S BATHROOM READER CLASSIC SERIES

Find these and other great titles from the *Uncle John's Bathroom Reader* Classic Series online at **www.bathroomreader.com**. Or contact us at:

Bathroom Readers' Institute
P.O. Box 1117 • Ashland, OR 97520 • (888) 488-4642

THE LAST PAGE

F**ELLOW BATHROOM READERS:**
The fight for good bathroom reading should never be taken loosely—
we must do our duty and sit firmly for what we believe in, even
while the rest of the world is taking potshots at us.

We'll be brief. Now that we've proven we're not simply a flush-in-the-pan, we invite you to take the plunge: Sit Down and Be Counted! Log on to *www.bathroomreader.com* and earn a permanent spot on the BRI honor roll!

If you like reading our books...
VISIT THE BRI'S WEB SITE!
www.bathroomreader.com

- Visit "The Throne Room"—a great place to read!
- Receive our irregular newsletters via e-mail
- Order additional *Bathroom Readers*
- Read our blog

Go with the Flow...

Well, we're out of space, and when you've gotta go, you've gotta go. Tanks for all your support. Hope to hear from you soon.

Meanwhile, remember...

Keep on flushin'!